WINNIE-THE-POOH
ON PROBLEM SOLVING

Winnie-the-Pooh

on Problem Solving

*In which
Pooh, Piglet, and friends
explore How to Solve Problems,
so you can too*

Roger E. Allen
and
Stephen D. Allen

A DUTTON BOOK

DUTTON
Published by the Penguin Group
Penguin Books USA Inc., 375 Hudson Street, New York, New York 10014, U.S.A.
Penguin Books Ltd, 27 Wrights Lane, London W8 5TZ, England
Penguin Books Australia Ltd, Ringwood, Victoria, Australia
Penguin Books Canada Ltd, 10 Alcorn Avenue, Toronto, Ontario, Canada M4V 3B2
Penguin Books (N.Z.) Ltd, 182–190 Wairau Road, Auckland 10, New Zealand
Penguin Books Ltd, Registered Offices: Harmondsworth, Middlesex, England

First published by Dutton, an imprint of Dutton Signet,
a division of Penguin Books USA Inc.
Distributed in Canada by McClelland & Stewart Inc.

First Printing, November, 1995
10   9   8   7   6   5   4   3

 REGISTERED TRADEMARK—MARCA REGISTRADA

LIBRARY OF CONGRESS CATALOGING-IN-PUBLICATION DATA
Allen, Roger E.
Winnie-the-Pooh on problem solving : in which Pooh, Piglet, and
friends explore how to solve problems so you can too / Roger E.
Allen and Stephen D. Allen.
ISBN: 0-525-94063-4
1. Problem solving.   I. Allen, Stephen D.   II. Title.
HD30.29.A45   1995   95-17641
153.4'3—dc20   CIP

Printed in the United States of America

The SOLVE problem-solving method copyright © Allen Associates, 1991.
Allen Associates Productivity Workshop.

To Fathers and Sons

ACKNOWLEDGMENTS

First and foremost, we should like to thank Alan Alexander Milne, and his son Christopher Robin Milne, without whose love and tenderness for each other, the world would be a bleaker place for want of a Certain Bear and his Friends.

Our thanks go out to the Milne estate for their kind approval and permission for the use of the excerpts and illustrations for this work.

We thank our editor, Matthew Carnicelli, for providing the guidance and editorial insight.

We thank our families for being there when needed and leaving us alone when isolation was required.

There are many people at Dutton that have helped create and produce this book, and while there are many we haven't met or don't know, we would like to thank

Joan Powers, PhD (Doctor of Poohology), Lisa Johnson and the entire Publicity department for their efforts on our behalf, especially Kate Cambridge, our publicist, and all the others who have lent their efforts.

CONTENTS

WINNIE-THE-POOH
ON PROBLEM SOLVING

INTRODUCTION

Not so very long ago a book was published which was called *Winnie-the-Pooh on Management: In which a Very Important Bear and his friends are introduced to a Very Important Subject*. (My, that is a *very* long title.)

Because some people read the book and some ever so kindly said they liked it and because there was more to say, it was decided to do another book. This one, that is.

This book is about how to solve problems. In the sense that solving problems is something that a manager often does and should be really good at doing, this book *could* be considered to be a continuation of *Winnie-the-Pooh on Management In which, etc., etc., etc.* However, this *is* a book for *everybody*, including managers.

You see, everyone has or will have problems. Success and/or happiness (defined however you like) depend to a considerable extent upon how well you solve the problems you take on and those that life presents to you.

The problem is, many people have problems with problems. Sometimes they don't solve a problem in the best way and end up with more problems or more serious problems. Many times they are not certain just how to solve the problem, where to start, or even what to do. As a result they do nothing, suffer the consequences of not solving it, or else limit their potential unnecessarily.

So, wouldn't it be great if there were a routine, easy way that problems could almost always be solved? A way that showed you where to start and step-by-step what to do? A way to solve a problem or improve a situation that you feel is less than satisfactory?

As you may have guessed, there *is* a way. We use it routinely in our consulting work (which consists for the most part of solving other people's problems). We think it is one of the most helpful things we know and use, in both our work and our personal lives, and we thought it would be a good thing to share.

So that is why this book was written.

Now, before we go any further, there are a few things we would like to explain for those who haven't read *Winnie-the-Pooh on Management In which* etc., etc., etc. (and you needn't have read it first to benefit from this book).

First, the adventures of Winnie-the-Pooh and friends (who very nicely gave us permission) were used because in our consulting work we found that people learned more easily and remembered better what was taught when we used their adventures. Much better than if we said, "This is the way Microsoft or McDonald's does it." Or, "This is how successful people do it." Psychologists call this technique placing material to be learned in an unfamiliar context. For instance, which is easier to remember? A weather forecaster saying, "The cumulative effect of atmospheric disturbances, fluctuating lows and highs, and the overall effect of the El Niño current will tend to result in alternating periods of precipitation and no precipitation," or the gloomy Eeyore observing, "Sometimes it rains and sometimes it doesn't. That's just the way it is."

Second, in *Winnie-the-Pooh on Management In which etc., etc., etc.*, Pooh meets The Stranger in the Hundred Acre Wood. The Stranger asks Pooh's help in writing a book about management basics. He is called "The Stranger" because that was the name Pooh thought of at the time, and it stuck even though it wasn't his real name. It is used again in this book because it is still sticking. As Winnie-the-Pooh, whose real name is Edward Bear, would say, "Some have nicknames and some haven't and there it is."

Finally, we thought we should have a shorter title for this book than you-know-what. It is our belief that a good title should tell someone standing in front of a book what the book is about. So *Winnie-the-Pooh on Problem Solving* was a logical choice.

When we had gotten to this point, Piglet looked up and complained that this book wasn't about him.

We told him that he was in the whole book and it *was* about him.

"So it is about Pooh," he squeaked. You see what it is. He is jealous because he thinks Pooh is having a Grand Introduction all to himself. Pooh is the favourite, of course, there's no denying it, but Piglet comes in for a good many things which Pooh misses: because you can't take Pooh to school without everybody knowing it, but Piglet is so small that he slips into a pocket, where it is very comfortable to feel him when you are not quite sure whether twice seven is twelve or twenty-two. Sometimes he slips out and has a good look in the ink-pot, and in this way he has got more education than Pooh, but Pooh doesn't mind. Some have brains, and some haven't he says, and there it is.

While we were explaining all this to Piglet, we were typing, and when we had finished we showed him the title of this book:

"Winnie-the-Pooh on Problem Solving In which Pooh, Piglet, and friends explore How to Solve Problems, so you can too." Which, although it isn't any shorter than *Winnie-the-Pooh on Management In which etc., etc., etc.,* does tell what the book is about.

"There's my name!" Piglet squeaked excitedly. "So the book *is* about me!"

This shows the value of an education—you can recognize your own name, especially when it is in the title of a book.

And now that we have solved Piglet's problem, we should stop writing introductions and get on with the book.

I

IN WHICH Winnie-the-Pooh Hosts a Gathering, The Stranger Returns to the Forest, and Almost Everyone Is Introduced to the SOLVE Problem-Solving Method

Everybody goes to Pooh's and almost everyone was at Pooh's. Of course, Christopher Robin was not and, as usual, Alexander Beetle was missing. Kanga had sent her regrets, but Tigger had brought Roo. Some of Rabbit's friends-and-relations may not have been there, but there were so many of them no one was really sure if they were or weren't. Piglet was particularly pleased that Small, who was one of the few individuals smaller than he was, had arrived riding on Eeyore's back.

Early that morning, Owl had swooped down from the sky to tell Pooh that he (Owl) had seen The Stranger getting off the train at the station in the village.

"Indisputably The Stranger is honoring the commitment he elucidated on the occasion of his departure to rendezvous with us at some indeterminate point in the future," Owl had explained.

"Oh," said Pooh as though he had understood what Owl said.

"He is walking in this direction and is carrying two large hampers," Owl added.

"Oh." Pooh understood that. "Two *large* hampers you say."

"Yes," said Owl. "If you agree, I'll go tell the others to come here to welcome The Stranger."

Pooh agreed that was a good idea, and began Straightening Things Up as Owl flew off. He paid particular attention to making certain that there was space on the larder shelves just in case The Stranger needed to leave whatever was left over from the large hampers at Pooh's. The last time The Stranger visited, he had brought honey, so Pooh had a particular interest in clearing his larder.

The Stranger came just after the last of the others had arrived, and Pooh was glad that Owl had been right. They were two *very* large hampers that The Stranger placed on the table.

Everyone's greetings and Hallos were made. Pooh made a very nice welcoming speech. When he had finished, The Stranger said he wanted to talk to them and ask them all a favor.

"There is a new book that I'm working on and I would like to ask you if I could use your adventures in writing it as I did with *Winnie-the-Pooh on Management*."

"What is it about?" Pooh asked. He was hoping that it might have been about management like the other book, which had said he was a V.I.B. (Very Important Bear).

"It's about Problem Solving."

"Prob . . . lem Solv . . . ing?" Pooh said slowly, scratching his head. "That sounds like a 'What.' 'Whats' are easy. It's the 'Hows' that are difficult. Will it be about the 'Hows' also?"

"Yes, Pooh," The Stranger answered. "It will show how almost anybody can become very good at finding solutions to problems or improving things."

"Even me?" squeaked Piglet. "I'm really not very good at solving problems. Often when there is a problem I get a headache or I try to go home. If I can, that is. With some problems you can't, you know. Like when Kanga thinks you are Roo and washes you and makes you take strengthening medicine."

Roo giggled. Piglet frowned to show that he didn't think that was very funny. Getting washed was a very serious subject and changed your color besides.

"Certainly, Piglet," The Stranger continued. "The book will teach a routine, easy way that anyone can use to solve problems or improve a situation. If any of you here in the forest would like to learn, you could do it while I'm working on the book."

"Is it important to know how to solve problems?" asked Pooh. He liked the idea of being a Very Important Bear, and if solving problems was important maybe it would help if he learned how. To solve problems that is.

"Very important. And it is becoming more and more so. Because of change and technology there are many new problems that need to be solved, that we've never had to solve before. That can be difficult because we can't say, 'Oh, that's just the same problem we solved last year.' We have to solve them without the benefit of experience. Examples of those would be the ones in the computer field and in communications and the Internet and DNA and—"

"That sounds about what one might expect," Eeyore interrupted. "Change almost always causes problems. I can remember when my house moved from one side of the pinewood to the other. It was very upsetting. Especially when I didn't know where it had moved to and it was snowing."

"We don't have much to do with things like ABC's and nets and things here in the Forest," said Rabbit. "Would this still help us?"

"Yes," said The Stranger. "This book will help with any kind of problem, old or new." The Stranger looked around the room. "May I use your adventures, and would you like to learn while I'm working on the book?"

"Yes," and "I'd like that," said Pooh and Piglet together. The others talked about whether it would be worth learning or not learning because once they solved their problems what could they use it for. Eeyore pointed out that it was unlikely that there would be a shortage of problems even if they all got very good at solving them. They all agreed that The Stranger should go ahead.

After he had thanked them, The Stranger said that if they didn't mind, he would like to get started and at least give them an idea about Problem Solving before they stopped for lunch.

Pooh minded, but since no one else said anything, he kept quiet.

"Well . . ." The Stranger began.

"I thought this was going to be about Problem Solving, not a hole in the ground," said Eeyore gloomily. "I might have known that I'd get it wrong."

"No, Eeyore," said The Stranger. "You didn't get it wrong. I just said 'Well' as a way to begin."

"Beginnings are almost always difficult," commented Pooh, frowning. "Sometimes beginnings start before you are ready for them and that can be a problem."

"Tiggers like solving problems," Tigger said cheerfully. "They are very good at it." Tigger looked thoughtful. "What *is* a problem?" he asked.

"That's a very good place to begin, Tigger," said The Stranger. "We'll start by talking about what a problem is."

Tigger bounced up and down three times, upsetting Piglet, who didn't like to be bounced on. "See," said Tigger. "Tiggers are good at this."

Piglet whispered something about extreme bounciness being considered a problem, especially when done by certain striped individuals, but Tigger didn't hear him.

"If we look at a dictionary," The Stranger continued, "we find that a problem is defined as 'a question proposed for a solution' and as 'a perplexing or difficult matter, person, or thing.' Can any of you give me an example of a problem?"

"Bounciness," said Piglet firmly. Louder this time.

"A tail that wants to be a bell pull," Eeyore added. "No sense of its proper place in life."

"How do you get honey from a Bee Tree?" Pooh said quickly, not wanting to be left out and also really wanting to know the solution. "That's a question proposed for a solution and it's also a perplexing and difficult matter if the bees don't want you to have it."

"Very good!" The Stranger beamed. "You've given three examples of very different problems. What is even better is that they can be used to point out one of the problems with problems and why so many individuals have difficulty solving the problems they encounter.

"You see, because problems often seem to be very different, it is natural to think that each one must be solved in a different way, and this really isn't the case at all."

"It isn't?" asked Owl, making certain that he was following the discussion. As he often said, the only problem with living in the Forest was that there was not much opportunity for intelligent discussions.

"No," The Stranger continued. "Over the years, ways have been developed to deal with problems using the same approach no matter how different the problems may be. These are called Problem-Solving Methods. Some of them have as many as ten steps, but the one we will use is one that was developed to be short, easy to use, and simple to remember. It is a five-step procedure called the SOLVE Problem-Solving Method."

"I don't understand," said Pooh slowly. "How does taking five steps solve the problem of say—ah—getting honey from the Bee Tree? In what direction do you take the steps?"

"It is inherently obvious that he is not referring to a numerical progression of ambulation, but rather to a number of actions that should be accomplished in a prescribed manner so as to effectively attack something that is bothersome with the objective of situational improvement or elimination," Owl explained.

"Oh," said Pooh, who didn't really understand anything that Owl had said, except the word "bothersome."

"Owl is correct," said The Stranger. "Putting it another way, we could say that the Problem-Solving Method is a list of things we should do in order to solve problems. What we should do first and what next and so on until we have solved the problem."

"Do you call it the SOLVE Method because it helps you to find the solutions to problems?" asked Owl, who was enjoying participating in the discussion and wanted to be certain he was holding up his end.

The Stranger nodded. "Partly for that reason, but also because it is an acronym for the steps that we follow in solving any problem."

Owl blinked his eyes and looked wise, which was very easy for him to do. He just wasn't sure what The Stranger had said SOLVE was. It had sounded as though he had said "A crow limb," but somehow Owl didn't think that was what he meant.

"What's an acro—acro—acro, what you said?" asked Roo, speaking up for the first time.

Since Roo was very young, everyone felt it was perfectly all right for him to ask the question. They all waited for the answer.

The Stranger looked pleased. "*Very* good, Roo," he said. "If there is something that you don't know or don't understand, always ask. Don't be afraid that others might think that you are not very smart. They might think that or make fun of you, but the fact that you asked shows that you are really intelligent."

"I was just about to ask," said Pooh, "but he beat me to it."

"Me too!" squeaked Piglet.

"I'm glad to hear that," The Stranger continued. "An acronym is a word formed from the first letters of several words. It is used so that you don't have to say all the words each time, and it is also a way to remind us what the words are that it stands for."

"So SOLVE really means something else," said Eeyore. "You might know. Anything to throw one off."

"Each letter of SOLVE stands for one of the steps that we need to take in order to solve a problem." The Stranger thought for a moment. "It is like going around in a circle.

"There is a problem, so you need or want to solve it.

Thinking of that reminds you of SOLVE, which in turn tells you exactly what you should do first and next and next until you find the solution."

"I think I see," said Pooh. "But I might understand it better if I knew what the words were that SOLVE stands for."

"I'll give them to you, but they won't mean much until we have had a chance to explain them in detail. However, we might as well start to learn them. In fact, I think I'll write them down." The Stranger walked over to the hampers he had brought, opened one, and took out a large tablet, an easel, and a pen.

Pooh was rather disappointed to see him do this because he had thought that the hampers were only for food. While The Stranger was setting up the easel along the wall where everyone could see it, Pooh peeked in the half-open basket and was relieved to see that it was still almost full of food.

"I'll write this down in the way that you will want to remember it," said The Stranger. This is what he wrote:

S elect the Problem or Situation.
O bserve, Organize, and Define the Problem or Situation.
L earn by Questioning All Parts of the Problem.
V isualize Possible Solutions, Select One, and Refine It.
E mploy the Solution and Monitor Results.

They all looked at it and then Piglet, who, except for The Stranger and Owl, was probably the best reader there, because of the many times he had gone to school in Christopher Robin's pocket, jumped up and down, squeaking, "Look! Look! If you read down only the first letter of each line you get S-O-L-V-E. That's SOLVE."

"Indisputally," said Owl, peering closely at what was written on the tablet. "I would venture to make the assumption that the remainder of the writing enscripted there comprises the steps that should be followed."

"Very good, Owl," said The Stranger. "You are exactly right."

"I think I understand the SOLVE idea," said Pooh. "But I don't understand the rest of it. I fear I am a Bear of Little Brain."

"Not at all," said The Stranger. "It's just that I haven't explained it yet. I promise you that you'll understand it when we use some of your adventures to make it clear."

"Oh," said Pooh, feeling somewhat better.

"First, however," The Stranger said, "it seems to me that it must be lunchtime. I think we'll learn better if we have a little something to eat before we continue."

"Oh, yes!" said Pooh, feeling much, much better.

The Stranger unpacked one of the hampers and put the food out on the table. "Pooh," he said, "since it is your house, why don't you start? Would you like to begin with some condensed milk or would you prefer honey?"

Pooh stood there, thinking about it.

Piglet, who had lined up behind him and was waiting for him to make up his mind, said, "That's a problem. You might even call it a Pooh-plexing problem. We might use that for a sample problem to use SOLVE on. After lunch, that is."

"No," said Pooh. "I've solved it. I'll start with both."

II

IN WHICH the Nature of Problems Is Explored and Tigger's, Rabbit's, and Piglet's Adventures Are Used As Examples

Lunch was over and Pooh had finished checking the hamper to make sure that there was nothing left that should be eaten so it wouldn't spoil. Everyone had helped in the cleaning up.

Pooh remembered that The Stranger had said that after lunch they would Explore and Explain just what problems were and were not.

Pooh felt very good about that because if there was anything in the way of words that were easy, it was X words. All you had to do was to find two straight sticks the same size in the Forest and put one on top of the other. Then you moved them around until they looked like an X. There wasn't much chance that it would be Wobbly. Then you added the rest of the word. If you cared to, that is.

Pooh settled down not too near the fireplace. Sitting too close tended to make him sleepy if he had just eaten.

The Stranger started to talk. "Does everyone remember what we decided a problem was?"

Everyone nodded and Owl spoke up. "We decided that it is a query propounded for exegesis culminating in a verbal expression of 'Eureka.' "

Pooh rather liked that and wished he had said it because it had two X words in it.

"Everything," said Eeyore gloomily. "But a tail is especially a problem. One that doesn't stay in its proper place."

"Very good," said The Stranger. "Remember that the dictionary defined a problem as 'A question proposed for a solution,' just—"

"That is precisely what I elucidated," interrupted Owl, looking sternly at The Stranger.

"Indeed it is," said The Stranger. "I was going to say . . . 'just as Owl said.' Very good, Owl."

"Oh," said Owl. "Thank you. One does try, you know."

Pooh wondered what had happened to 'Exegesis' but didn't get a chance to ask before The Stranger continued.

"My dictionary also defined a problem as 'a difficult matter, person, or thing' . . ."

"Just what I said," muttered Eeyore. " 'Everything' covers all that, you know. But do you think I'd get credit? Not very likely. But there you are."

". . . which is what Eeyore's 'everything' implied," finished The Stranger.

"Credit where credit is due," said Eeyore. "Better late than never, I suppose."

"Now that we have reviewed what a problem is," The Stranger continued, "let's see what we can learn about the nature of problems. Pooh, before lunch you said getting honey was a problem."

"Yes," said Pooh, and just in case The Stranger was going to solve it right now, he added, "Getting honey, and getting enough, every time. Which is often."

The Stranger turned to Tigger. "Is getting honey a problem for you?" he asked.

Tigger thought for a moment. "No." He shook his head and his tail at the same time just to lend emphasis to his answer. Tiggers are very good at doing that.

"Why do you say that?" asked The Stranger.

"Because I remember when I first came to the Forest, I went to Pooh's house. It was the middle of the night and Pooh heard me, got out of bed, and opened his front door."

"I thought he might be a Strange Animal," said Pooh. "Making a noise of some kind. I got up to ask him not to do it."

"I remember that," said The Stranger. "Here it is in the book I brought along. I'll read it."

"Hallo!" said Pooh, in case there was anything outside.

"Hallo!" said Whatever-it-was.

"Oh!" said Pooh. "Hallo!"

"Hallo!"

"Oh *there* you are!" said Pooh. "Hallo!"

"Hallo!" said the Strange Animal, wondering how long this was going on.

Pooh was just going to say "Hallo" for the fourth time when he thought he wouldn't, so he said: "Who is it?" instead.

"Me," said a voice.

"Oh!" said Pooh. "Well, come here."

So Whatever-it-was came here and in the light of the candle he and Pooh looked at each other.

"I'm Pooh," said Pooh.

"I'm Tigger," said Tigger.

"Oh!" said Pooh, for he had never seen an animal like this before. "Does Christopher Robin know about you?"

"Of course he does," said Tigger.

"Well," said Pooh, "it's the middle of the night, which is a good time for going to sleep. And tomorrow morning we'll have some honey for breakfast. Do Tiggers like honey?"

"They like everything," said Tigger cheerfully.

"So I went back to bed," said Pooh, "and Tigger slept on the floor."

"In the morning a tablecloth tried to bite me when I wasn't looking," said Tigger, "but I was too quick for it."

The Stranger ran his finger down the page until he found the proper place.

Pooh put the cloth back on the table, and he put a large honey-pot on the cloth, and they sat down to breakfast. And as soon as they sat down, Tigger took a large mouthful of honey . . . and he looked up at the ceiling with his head on one side, and made exploring noises with his tongue and considering noises, and what-have-we-got-*here* noises . . . and then he said in a very decided voice:

"Tiggers don't like honey."

"Oh!" said Pooh, and tried to make it sound Sad and Regretful. "I thought they liked everything."

"Everything except honey," said Tigger.

"So that's why getting honey is not a problem for me," said Tigger. "I don't like honey."

"So what can we learn about problems from Tigger?" asked The Stranger.

The room was very quiet while everyone thought about what their answer might be.

At first Pooh thought that the answer might be that he would have less of a problem getting honey if everyone was like Tigger because there would be more honey to go around and the only one to go around it would be Pooh. "Ummmmmmm," he thought. But he must have thought it out loud because Owl, who was perched next to him, turned his head and peered at him and asked him if lunch had not agreed with him because he was making a strange sound.

Pooh decided that his first thought was probably not what The Stranger wanted, even though it was a good thought.

Pooh liked honey, so getting it was a problem. Tigger didn't like it, so getting honey was not a problem for him.

"What . . . is . . . a . . . problem . . . for . . . one," Pooh said very slowly, "maynotbeaproblemforanother." He finished in a rush to get his Thought out before he forgot.

"Very good, Pooh!" The Stranger said excitedly. "That is exactly right, and everyone should remember that it is a very important aspect of the nature of problems. Deciding whether something is or is not a problem is a personal decision. While many things are considered to be a problem by almost all of us, it remains that the determination that something is a problem, or how serious it is, can vary from individual to individual. We say that problems are Steeped in Perceptions."

"Like the time we were trying to unbounce Tigger so we took him up to the top of the Forest, so he'd get lost and be less bouncy," Piglet piped up. "Pooh and Rabbit and I got lost in the mist, and we all thought being lost was a problem. Even Christopher Robin was anxious. But Tigger didn't think getting lost was a problem so he just went back to Kanga's, where he and Roo had dinner."

"I remember that," squeaked Roo, pleased that something he had done was being mentioned. "We played at fir cones too. But I forget how it ended."

"It ended like this," said Piglet.

And it was just as they were finishing dinner that Christopher Robin put his head in at the door.

"Where's Pooh?" he asked.

"Tigger dear, where's Pooh?" said Kanga. Tigger explained what had happened at the same time that Roo was explaining about his biscuit cough and Kanga was telling them not both to talk at once, so it was some time before Christopher Robin guessed that Pooh and Piglet and Rabbit were all lost in the mist at the top of the Forest.

"It's a funny thing about Tiggers," whispered Tigger to Roo, "how Tiggers *never* get lost."

"Why don't they, Tigger?"

"They just don't," explained Tigger. "That's how it is."

"So we can see from Pooh's problem with honey that individuals may vary in thinking that something is a problem," pointed out The Stranger, "and from Piglet's that everyone may think something is a problem but one individual may not. That's why we say that the determination that something is a problem is a subjective one.

"In addition, problems can often be insidious and may not even seem to be a problem at first," The Stranger continued. "They can come to you in a form that is difficult to recognize or disguised as something else."

"Like a gorse bush," said Pooh. "It looks like a harmless bush, but when you fall in it you get prickles in your nose and other parts, which is most unpleasant. Gorse bushes can be problems."

"Very much like that," agreed The Stranger. "In addition, sometimes problems have emotional associations that make them more difficult to solve. For example, if there is an element of fear associated with the problem . . ."

"Like trying to find your way home through the Forest and meeting a Heffalump with no one around to help, and you can't run because the snow is so deep and it's dark . . ." Piglet's voice was going higher and higher as he imagined a more and more fearsome situation. "And it is freezing and there might be two Heffalumps, one ahead of you and one close behind and they haven't eaten anything for days and . . ." Piglet ran out of breath and had to stop.

"It can make it difficult to concentrate on how you can find your way home," The Stranger finished for him.

Piglet shivered. "I would not want to have that problem. I'd wait until there were no Heffalumps around before I'd try to find the way home."

"That's called procrastination," said The Stranger.

"It means putting off doing something that you should do," said Owl, seeing the puzzled look on Pooh's face.

"Oh," said Pooh. "I thought he said 'poohcrastination.' Thank you, Owl."

"Many individuals do just that when they are faced with a problem," said The Stranger. "The problem with procrastination is that while you are avoiding facing up to the problem, it might get worse."

"A third Heffalump might come along," said Eeyore. "They often travel in threes, or so I've heard."

"Oooo!" said Piglet, sorry that he had thought up this example of a problem. He looked quickly around the room, just to make certain that there were no shadowy places where a Heffalump or three might be hiding, waiting to jump out at a passing Piglet. There were none, so he moved over closer to Pooh and settled down to listen to The Stranger.

"All emotions and all attitudes can have an effect on the process of Problem Solving and can have an influence on how satisfactory your solution may be. Often your emotions can make you think there is a problem when there really isn't. A good example of that was your adventure when Kanga and Baby Roo came to the forest."

"I remember that," said Rabbit.

"Me too! I remember too!" piped Roo.

"We thought that Kangas were Generally Regarded as One of the Fiercer Animals," said Pooh.

"They were different so we wanted them to leave the Forest," said Rabbit.

"But they were really very nice and now they are our friends so there wasn't a problem after all," said Piglet.

"Exactly," said The Stranger. "That is why we must always be very careful to be aware of the possible effect that attitudes and emotions may have on problems we are trying to solve. Sometimes individuals working on a problem will say something like, 'Let's get an unbiased opinion.' That means they want to be sure that emotions are not affecting the problem or the solution, so they get someone who hasn't been involved to review their work. Sometimes this is called getting a Fresh Perspective."

Pooh practiced saying "Fresh Perspective" under his breath several times, since he liked the sound of it. It sounded like the sort of thing that Owl might very well say. It ended up as "Fresh Poohspective," which was all right because he liked it just as well. Maybe even better.

"Is that all there is about the nature of problems?" asked Tigger, who had been restraining his bounciness for a long time.

"I'm afraid not, Tigger," answered The Stranger. "There is one more aspect of problems that I would like to talk about before we finish for the day."

Tigger bounced twice very quickly so that no one saw him. It relieved some of his bounciness, so he could listen as The Stranger continued.

"I wanted to mention that problems often don't come

one at a time. Frequently you are faced with several that you have to solve at the same time, or in a certain order. Can anyone think of one of your adventures where that was the case?"

"The adventure In Which Piglet Does a Very Grand Thing was like that," said Pooh.

"That's a good one, Pooh. Why don't you tell us about it."

"That was the day that it was very Blusterous," said Pooh, "and Piglet and I were going to Owl's house to have a Proper Tea with him."

The wind was against them now and Piglet's ears

streamed behind him

like banners

as he fought his way along, and it seemed hours be- fore he got them into the shelter of the Hundred Acre

Wood and they stood up straight again, to listen, a little nervously, to the roaring of the gale among the tree-tops.

"Supposing a tree fell down, Pooh, when we were underneath it?"

"Supposing it didn't," said Pooh after careful thought.

"I think I remember," said The Stranger. "A tree did fall down, didn't it?"

"Yes," said Pooh. "But we weren't underneath it. We were in it."

"It was Owl's tree," said Piglet. "It was just as you said. There were a number of problems . . . all at one time."

"We couldn't go out by what used to be the front door," said Owl. "Something had fallen on it. Getting out was a problem."

"I was in a very uncomfortable position. Fallen downward under something with someone asking me to look at the ceiling, as I remember," said Pooh. "That was the first problem."

"And then there was how I was to get up to the letter box without falling and seriously damaging myself." Piglet shivered, just remembering.

"To say nothing of my no longer having a house," Owl said. "Being homeless is never easy and is almost always a problem."

"I know," said Eeyore gloomily. "From sad experience. But it *is* what one expects. Especially if it is cold and snowy out."

"That's a perfect example of what I was talking about," said The Stranger.

"How did they ever solve all those problems?" squeaked Roo, who always wanted to know how things turned out.

If Kanga had been there she would have said, "Now Roo, Dear, just wait. You'll find out in due time."

The Stranger said much the same thing only using different words. "If you don't mind, Roo, we'll find out later. Now while it's all fresh in our minds I'd like to summarize what we've learned about the nature of problems."

We have said that whether something is considered a problem is subjective, and the perception of its seriousness might vary from individual to individual. Problems can sometimes come to us disguised, or appearing to be something that they are not. The way we approach and solve a problem may be influenced by our own or other people's emotional factors or attitudes. Problems can be simple or complex. There may be more than one problem that we are faced with at a time, or we may have to solve problems in a certain order."

The Stranger stopped and looked around the room. "Does anyone have any questions?" He waited a moment. "If no one has, then I think we have covered enough for the day. I suggest we see what's in that second hamper."

What was there was enough for a Very Fine Tea, with enough left over for an evening meal.

While they were having their tea everyone told Roo how all the problems had been solved when Owl's house was blown down, and he fell asleep just as Pooh finished telling about the Very Grand Thing that Piglet did.

III

In which It Is Shown that SOLVE Is Not Just for Problems and Eeyore Endures a Moving Experience

Almost everyone was already there when The Stranger came by the next morning and arrived at Pooh's house. Small had gotten lost again and Rabbit was out looking for him, so they weren't there. Kanga had once more begged off as having to do housework she had been procrastinating about ("See," said Pooh to Piglet. "We were warned about that."), but she sent Roo along with Tigger. Alexander Beetle was still missing and some thought he might have buried himself head downward in a crack in the ground as he sometimes did.

"That's not altogether a bad thing," said Eeyore almost cheerfully. "Then one doesn't have to be careful all the time not to step or sit on him."

"Or Small," piped up Piglet. "Because he's not here too. Or is it 'here also' and 'sit on them'?"

"Or Small," Eeyore agreed. "Whatever."

Since it had been late the night before by the time the storytelling was over and Roo had fallen asleep, Pooh had ever so nicely offered to let The Stranger sleep on the floor of his house. But The Stranger told Pooh that he felt it would be an imposition, and he would stay at the inn in the village that was only about a mile down the road. Really just a pleasant stroll. He said he would see everyone in the morning, and they would talk about a different kind of problem.

After he had left, Piglet asked Pooh, "What's an 'imposition'?"

Pooh thought for a moment. "I think it has something to do with the way he curls up on the floor."

"Oh," said Piglet. "I just wondered."

When he came in, The Stranger apologized for being late and said that because of that he wanted to start right away.

"What I want to talk about," The Stranger began, "is that the SOLVE Method is not just for problems. Yesterday, we talked about problems and difficulties that you have had in your adventures. Finding breakfast for Tigger, getting lost in the mist at the top of the Forest, and Owl's house being blown down were all problems or difficulties you had experienced. The SOLVE Method will help with those problems. However, the SOLVE Method can *also* be a powerful way to improve situations or things that you choose."

The Stranger pointed to the tablet, which was still on

the easel against the wall. "You will remember that the first step of the SOLVE Method says 'Select the Problem or Situation.' Let me explain why the word 'Situation' is there."

"I wondered about that," said Eeyore. "I thought this was all about Problem Solving. I haven't heard anything about 'situation solving.' Adding on and confusing things just at the last minute is not helpful." He shook his head. "Not at all helpful."

"The reason we add 'Situation' to our Select step," explained The Stranger, "instead of just saying 'Select the Problem,' is that selection can be either a passive process or an active one.

"Passive choices are usually ones that are presented to you for solving, often by somebody else or by fate. A family member, a friend, your boss, your country or where you live, economic conditions, illness and so on, can all present you with problems that you need to solve. You were passive. The problem came to you. You didn't have to do anything to be put into the position of needing to solve it. A good example of a passive choice is the one we talked about, when the wind blew down Owl's house.

"On the other hand . . ."

"He means 'As distinguished from the first thing he was talking about,'" Pooh whispered to Piglet. Pooh had learned that from Owl, but he wasn't certain that Piglet knew.

"Thank you, Pooh," said Piglet. "I wasn't sure."

". . . active choices are the ones that you consciously make, usually in an effort to improve or make something better. The way you do it is, you decide to treat a situation as if it were a problem, even though it may not be one at the moment, and apply the SOLVE Method to it to improve it.

"As you get good at solving problems, you'll find yourself selecting situations for improvement more and more frequently. That's why we added 'Situation' to the Select step."

Eeyore shook his head at this. "I don't think I understand," he said. "It seems to me that there are enough problems to solve without going out and making things problems that aren't. Problems, that is."

The Stranger thought for a moment. "Let me give you an example and see if it makes things clearer. Let's use the time when Pooh and Piglet decided to help you. You remember, it went like this:"

"I've been thinking," said Pooh, "and what I've been thinking is this. I've been thinking about Eeyore."

"What about Eeyore?"

"Well, poor Eeyore has nowhere to live."

"Nor he has," said Piglet.

"You have a house, Piglet, and I have a house, and they are very good houses. And Christopher Robin has a house, and Owl and Kanga and Rabbit have houses, and even Rabbit's friends and relations have houses or somethings, but poor Eeyore has nothing. So what I've been thinking is: Let's build him a house."

"That," said Piglet, "is a Grand Idea. Where shall we build it?"

"We will build it here," said Pooh, "just by this wood out of the wind, because this is where I thought of it. And we will call this Pooh Corner. And we will build an Eeyore House with sticks at Pooh Corner for Eeyore."

"There was a heap of sticks on the other side of the wood," said Piglet. "I saw them. Lots and lots. All piled up."

"Thank you, Piglet," said Pooh. "What you have just said will be a Great Help to us, and because of it I could call this place Poohanpiglet Corner if Pooh Corner didn't sound better, which it does, being smaller and more like a corner. Come along."

So they got down off the gate and went around to the other side of the wood to fetch the sticks.

"I see what you mean," said Eeyore. "About making something a problem when it wasn't one in order to improve it. I had built myself a house and when I had left it in the morning, it was there. When I came back, it was gone. So that was a problem. It wasn't really gone. It had just been moved to the other side of the wood. I decided the wind had done it."

"But you said the house was better in places," said Pooh.

"And we said 'Much better,'" said Piglet.

"And that means it was improved," said The Stranger, who was a little embarrassed because he had forgotten that Eeyore had built himself a house that Pooh and Piglet didn't know about. So when Pooh and Piglet decided to build him one they used the house Eeyore had built to build the new one. Eeyore hadn't been told this and he still thought the wind had done it.

"I see," said Eeyore. "Pooh and Piglet made my house a problem even though it wasn't and it ended up improved."

"Yes," said Pooh and Piglet at the same time.

"In any event," The Stranger said, "things or situations that aren't problems can be improved by saying they are a problem and using SOLVE as if they were a problem."

Owl, who read the *Wall Street Journal*, looked wise and said, "I frequently see in the paper where companies are improving their costs in a particular area, or are developing an improved version of their product even though there was nothing wrong with the old one. So this would be a way to do that."

"Exactly," said The Stranger, "and individuals can use SOLVE to upgrade their skills or improve something about themselves or their situation that they find unsatisfactory."

"Like bounciness," said Piglet.

"I already bounce about as well as I can," said Tigger, "but maybe I could work out a way to go higher."

"Not what I meant," muttered Piglet, but Tigger didn't hear him.

"Kanga bounces higher than you do," Roo said helpfully. "Maybe she could give you lessons or you could use SOLVE to bounce even higher."

Piglet shuddered at the thought.

The Stranger said, "I think it might be almost time to have lunch. Let me review one more thing and then we'll see if the inn gave us good food in the picnic basket which I left outside so it would stay cool."

Everyone agreed that was a good idea.

"One thing that I want to stress. We decided that the nature of problems that came to you was that they could be simple or complex, single or multiple, subjective or come to you disguised, and that emotional factors or attitudes of yours or of those involved can affect your solutions and how you deal with problems.

"Now, the nature of the situations that you select yourself in order to improve them is exactly the same as the problems that are presented to you. The only difference between the two types of problems in the way you use SOLVE is in the S step, which we'll talk about after lunch."

"What I still don't understand," said Eeyore to Piglet while they were waiting for the picnic basket to be unpacked, "is how you and Pooh's deciding to build me a house ended up improving my house when the wind moved it."

"Probably we'll learn about that when The Stranger teaches us about the five steps of SOLVE," said Piglet carefully.

"The way things usually are," said Eeyore gloomily, "I probably still won't know even when we are all finished."

"I think that's possible," Piglet said. At least I hope so, he added to himself.

IV

In which the Select Step Is
Discussed, Pooh Learns Right from
Wrong, and Piglet Discovers
His Name

"So far we have spent our time on the nature of problems,"
The Stranger began. "Now we will begin to talk about the
way to solve problems.

"In order to use our SOLVE Method, we must have a
problem for which we want to find a solution. That is the
first step of our five-step method—to Select the Problem
that we will work on.

"We must take care in this first step because, as we
discussed, problems sometimes come to us disguised. Problems are like what Sir Winston Churchill—"

"Another Winnie!" said Pooh proudly.

"—like what Sir Winston Churchill said about Russia,"
continued The Stranger. "It is 'a riddle wrapped in a mys-
tery inside an enigma.' We want to be sure we pick the
right problem to work on."

Everyone looked at him blankly. Pooh didn't even say, "Oh, I see," which he usually said even when he didn't.

"Maybe a better way to stress that point," The Stranger said, "is to use the adventure when Kanga and Roo came to the Forest. They were new and everyone thought it was a bad thing because they were supposed to be one of the Fiercer Animals. It was decided that the problem was how to get them to leave the Forest."

As The Stranger was saying this, Roo was doing his best trying to look like one of the Fiercer Animals, but he didn't do very well, because Tigger thought he was trying to have a Funny Face Contest and made a face, making Roo begin to giggle. This, of course, ruined the effect because it is well known that the Fiercer Animals do not generally giggle.

"I remember," Piglet piped up. "The problem really was that we didn't know enough about Kanga and Roo to decide if they were a problem or not. All we knew was what they looked like, and I know *now* that sometimes mistakes are made based on appearance. It happened to me, because I was pretending to be Roo so we could kidnap Roo and scare Kanga into leaving the Forest. And Christopher Robin came by and didn't know I was me, because I looked different."

"I don't think I remember that," said The Stranger. "What happened?"

"It was just after Kanga gave me a cold water bath and strengthening medicine because I was supposed to be Roo and Christopher Robin came by. I tried to tell him that I was Piglet.

Christopher Robin shook his head again.

"Oh you're not Piglet," he said. "I know Piglet well, and he's *quite* a different colour."

Piglet began to say that this was because he had just had a bath, and then he thought that perhaps he wouldn't say that, and as he opened his mouth to say something else, Kanga slipped the medicine spoon in, and then patted him on the back and told him that it was really quite a nice taste when you got used to it.

"I knew it wasn't Piglet," said Kanga. "I wonder who it can be."

"Perhaps it's some relation of Pooh's," said Christopher Robin. "What about a nephew or an uncle or something?"

Kanga agreed that this was probably what it was, and said that they would have to call it by some name.

"I shall call it Pootel," said Christopher Robin. "Henry Pootel for short."

And just when it was decided, Henry Pootel wriggled out of Kanga's arms and jumped to the ground. To his great joy Christopher Robin had left the door open. Never had Henry Pootel Piglet run so fast as he ran then, and he didn't stop running until he had got quite close to his house. But when he was a hundred yards away he stopped running, and rolled the rest of the way home, so as to get his own nice comfortable colour again.

"And that was how I found out my full name," said Piglet. "Henry Pootel Piglet. That meant I had the same number of names as Edward Pooh Bear." Piglet paused. "As long as you don't count the 'Winnie-the-' part, that is."

"That certainly shows that mistakes can be made if you just go by appearance," said The Stranger. "When you are selecting a problem, you must be careful that you have selected the problem you want or need to solve. As Phaedrus wrote, 'Things are not always what they seem.'"

"Who is Phaedrus?" asked Owl, who liked to know about things like that.

"He was a Macedonian writer who lived almost two thousand years ago," said The Stranger, who also liked to know about things like that.

"That's a long time ago," said Piglet. "I wonder if things are always what they seem now."

Owl was blinking his eyes very rapidly because he was saying, "Phaedrus, Phaedrus, Phaedrus" to himself, so he would remember it in case he was ever asked.

"Now," The Stranger continued, "our first step in the five-step SOLVE Method is the S step. Who remembers what it stands for?"

"S stands for Select the Problem or Situation," said Piglet, looking at the tablet that was still on the easel.

The Stranger nodded approvingly. "Sometimes selecting the problem is easy and obvious, but, because of the nature of problems, we must always give some thought to making certain that we have selected the right problem."

"The way things usually are," said Eeyore gloomily, "I probably will pick the wrong problem. Why is that bad?"

"I think," said Pooh, "that if you don't pick the right problem, it's the wrong problem which means that you still have to solve the right problem after you've solved the wrong problem, if you do. Right?"

Everyone thought about what Pooh had said and after they had worked out the rights and the wrongs, decided that he was right.

"That's right, Pooh," said The Stranger, "but it's only half of the reason."

"So we need another half," squeaked Piglet. When he had gone to school in Christopher Robin's pocket once, he had been exposed to higher mathematics. Christopher Robin had taken him out of his pocket and he had seen written on the blackboard $\frac{1}{2} + \frac{1}{2} = 1$. After school Christopher Robin had explained it to him using a stick he had broken in the middle. Piglet was excited because now was his chance to make use of what he had learned.

"Yes," said Owl. "What is the remaining portion of the integer?"

"If we select the wrong problem," The Stranger explained, "as well as wasting our time and efforts, in some cases we may also limit our choice of possible solutions to the situation we find ourselves in."

"I don't understand," said Eeyore. "See, I told you I'd have trouble with this problem-solving thing. Maybe I should just give up." He shook his head. "Pathetic. That's what it is. Pathetic."

"No, Eeyore," said The Stranger. "Don't feel discouraged about having trouble. That only means that you may have to work harder, but in the end you'll learn it better. One of the world's greatest inventors, Charles F. Kettering, said, 'Don't bring me anything but trouble. Good news weakens me.' So don't worry, Eeyore, and *don't* give up. Another famous man, Thomas J. Watson, Sr., the founder of IBM, said, 'Success is on the far side of failure.' Now let me see if I can explain about how selecting the wrong problem can limit your chances for a satisfactory solution. In the case of Kanga and Roo, it was decided that they were strange and were Generally Regarded as Two of the Fiercer Animals, and the problem was that they were there in the Forest."

"Mostly it was Rabbit who decided," said Pooh.

"We decided also," said Piglet quickly, wanting to make sure that he got some of the credit if there was any.

"By deciding wrongly that the problem was that Kanga and Roo were in the Forest—" began The Stranger.

"Mostly it was Rabbit," Piglet interrupted quickly, "who decided, that is."

"—the only solution that comes to mind is to get them out of the Forest."

"Makes sense to me," said Eeyore.

"However, by picking the right problem—that you don't know enough about these new animals—all sorts of solutions are made possible. You can learn more about them. Find out if they really are Two of the Fiercer Animals. See if they could live only in a portion of the Forest. Set up a test period to let them stay and see if there are any problems. Learn if they might be good friends and on and on. There are probably a dozen or more solutions when you pick the right problem versus only one in this case if you pick the wrong problem."

"I see now," said Eeyore. "Thank you. That is much clearer."

"Good," said The Stranger. "At this point in our S step we want to decide and think about several things before we go on.

"The first is whether the problem selected you, or you selected the problem or situation. While you proceed with SOLVE in the same manner in both cases, if the problem selected you, you might want to review it to make certain you are working on the right problem.

"Second, evaluate if the problem is simple or complex and if it is a single problem or a multiple one. As we have discussed, if it is multiple, you will have to consider the order of working on the problems and their relative priorities, particularly in the O step.

"Thirdly, think and evaluate if the problem or situation has any emotional factors involved. Sometimes the problem or situation does and sometimes the individuals involved will have emotional associations either with the problem or with others who are involved."

"You mean . . . like if there is a Heffalump involved?" asked Piglet. "And someone who was afraid of Heffalumps was involved."

"Yes. That would be an example, but it doesn't necessarily have to be a negative emotion like fear or anger. You could have a case where the problem involved two other people and you liked one much better than the other.

That could affect the way you approach the problem and your solution."

"So what do you do," asked Owl, "if you find there are emotional factors involved?"

"Sometimes you can't do very much except be aware that they are there and very carefully examine your work to see that the emotional factors don't unduly influence you.

"As the final part of the S step, you should state the problem or situation as clearly and simply as you can. If you can't do this easily, it may be that either you don't understand the problem, or you may have selected the wrong problem. I often find it helpful to see if I can write what the problem is on one side of a single piece of paper. If you have difficulty at this point you should go back and rethink what the problem is, or clarify what you don't understand."

The Stranger paused and looked out the window, where it was beginning to get dark.

"Before we finish for the day I want to cover one more thing.

"You will remember that we said that SOLVE is not just for Problem Solving. It can be used for improving something that may not be a problem."

"Yes," said Eeyore. "I wondered about that. It seems to me it might be difficult to decide what should be improved since everything that isn't a problem right now might be improved. Which means there is more than one thing, maybe even three or four, that you need to decide about." Eeyore looked around the room. "I think."

"There are no specific rules, Eeyore," said The Stranger, "but you're right. It sometimes *is* difficult to pick out where to use SOLVE. It is mostly a matter of judgment, but there are some general guidelines. They are: Pick something that you think could be improved."

"Like a tail," said Eeyore.

"Yes," said The Stranger. "Or someone might want to look better, or lose a little weight."

"I did that once when I got stuck in the door of Rabbit's house," said Pooh. "I wouldn't want to do that again."

"Some people might want to save more money or improve the skills they use either at work or in their personal life," The Stranger continued.

"At work or on the job it's a little easier to decide what to improve. You select situations where there is lots of money or time involved, where safety is a factor, or to improve service to your customers or clients.

"In the end, it's mostly a matter of your judgment. If you do pick something to improve when something else might have been a better choice, you still will have improved something.

"Are there any questions on the S step of SOLVE?" he asked.

"No," said Pooh, after a minute or so of concentration. "I believe it is all straight in my Brain. I think I understand." The others agreed, except for Tigger, who was stalking a beetle who turned out to be Alexander, who had gotten trapped under the rug the last time he had visited Pooh's.

"Well, if that's the case," said The Stranger, "I think we have covered enough for today. Next time we shall learn to Observe, Organize, and Define Problems. Would meeting next Tuesday to talk about the O step of SOLVE be all right?"

"No problem," everyone said in chorus, except for Tigger, who had just bounced on Alexander before he recognized who he was.

V

IN WHICH Everyone Observes (the Second Step in the SOLVE Method), Tigger and Roo Are Stuck, and Pooh Hums a New Hum

"Hallo, Pooh!" said The Stranger.

"Happy Tuesday," said Pooh, hoping that it really was Tuesday but not being entirely sure.

"Happy Tuesday!" chimed Piglet and Eeyore and Tigger and Roo.

The Stranger set down the briefcase he had been carrying and looked at Pooh's friends thoughtfully.

"Well, well, well. I didn't know all of you were going to be here today or I would have brought along lunch."

Pooh worried, especially as he had eaten only a bit for his elevenses before gathering his friends together to meet with The Stranger. "You did say that we were going to meet and learn to Observe, Organize, and Define Problems."

"So I did, and so we shall. What did you think that meant?"

"Well," Pooh said, "when Christopher Robin was observing his birthday, it meant getting everyone together and having little cake things with pink sugar icing and singing songs. So when you said we would be observing, I made sure to ask everyone to come."

"But Kanga and Owl and Rabbit couldn't come," said Eeyore. "So they'll be the only dry ones once it starts to rain. Which it will do any moment now."

"I see," said The Stranger, chuckling. "Well, the type of observing I had in mind is not quite like that . . ."

Pooh began to worry even more about Needing a Little Something to keep up his strength.

". . . but perhaps we can have some fun anyway. I am glad you all could come along to listen. It's a bit cold this morning, so let's see if we can get a nice warm fire going. I think we can get started if you'll just help me."

"I can! I will!" squeaked Piglet, who began running back and forth looking for sticks and twigs for the fire while The Stranger collected some stones and rocks for a fire ring.

Pooh's worrying went away when the fire crackled to life and bright warmth spread out and enveloped him.

"This kind of observing seems a lot like the other so far," said Pooh, "except for the little cake things with pink sugar icing."

"At least until it starts pouring," said Eeyore, eyeing the dark clouds above.

"Tiggers like it when it rains," offered Tigger, looking up at the sky and bouncing expectantly.

"The type of observing I was going to explain today is the second step in solving problems," The Stranger said. "You remember yesterday we talked about selecting a problem and how some of them you choose and sometimes they choose you."

"Like when Tigger and Roo became stuck in the tallest Pine Tree," squeaked Piglet.

"That's right," said The Stranger. Piglet beamed, remembering how he and Pooh had been walking in the Forest. . . .

"Look, Pooh!" said Piglet suddenly. "There's something in one of the Pine Trees."

"So there is!" said Pooh, looking up wonderingly. "There's an Animal."

Piglet took Pooh's arm, in case Pooh was frightened.

"Is it One of the Fiercer Animals?" he said, looking the other way.

Pooh nodded.

"It's a Jagular," he said.

"What do Jagulars do?" asked Piglet, hoping that they wouldn't.

"They hide in the branches of trees, and drop on you as you go underneath," said Pooh. "Christopher Robin told me."

"Perhaps we better hadn't go underneath, Pooh. In case he dropped and hurt himself."

"They don't hurt themselves," said Pooh. "They're such very good droppers."

Piglet still felt that to be underneath a Very Good Dropper would be a Mistake, and he was just going to hurry back for something which he had forgotten when the Jagular called out to them.

"Help! Help!" it called.

"That's what Jagulars always do," said Pooh, much interested. "They call 'Help! Help!' and then when you look up, they drop on you."

"I'm looking *down*," cried Piglet loudly, so as the Jagular shouldn't do the wrong thing by accident.

Something very excited next to the Jagular heard him, and squeaked:

"Pooh and Piglet! Pooh and Piglet!"

All of a sudden Piglet felt that it was a much nicer day than he had thought it was. All warm and sunny—

"Pooh!" he cried. "I believe it's Tigger and Roo!"

"So it is," said Pooh. "I thought it was a Jagular and another Jagular."

"We can't get down, we can't get down!" cried Roo. . . .

"Are they stuck?" asked Piglet anxiously.

Pooh nodded.

"So the problem was that they were stuck in the Tree," said The Stranger.

"And that they weren't Jagulars," squeaked Piglet, "because they are Very Good Droppers and could have just dropped down if they were."

"And landed on you," added Eeyore. Piglet squirmed.

"Once we have decided what the problem is," said The Stranger, "in this case, that Tigger and Roo were stuck up in the Tree, the next step is to Observe the problem or situation, Organize the different parts, and begin to Define them.

"We do this by deciding where things are now, where we would like them to be—which would be our goal—and by noticing anything that might be in the way of achieving our goal." The Stranger paused for a moment to use a long stick to stir up the embers of the fire before continuing. "We've said that Tigger and Roo were stuck far up in the tallest Pine Tree. That is a good statement of where things were. Next we would look at where we would like them to be."

"On the ground," said Tigger, remembering what the Forest looked like from so high.

"So we could say that the goal was to get you and Roo back down onto the ground."

"But that's not all," said Pooh. "Not being Jagulars, dropping would be out of the question."

"That's exactly right, Pooh," said The Stranger. *That* kind of bear, thought Pooh. "And that is an example of something that is in the way."

"Like me," said Eeyore.

"No, Eeyore. Something that is in the way of solving the problem satisfactorily, which is called a constraint."

"Like Tigger's not being able to climb down backward," added Roo.

"That's right," said The Stranger. "So a constraint is something that keeps you from accomplishing your goal, or that complicates the solution of the problem."

"Bees are constraints," said Pooh, rubbing his nose and remembering how complicated it had been trying to get honey from the Bee Tree because of them.

"Yes," said The Stranger, "I can see that they might be a particularly painful sort of constraint for a bear. Constraints usually reduce or dictate the possible solutions or the options you have as to how you can solve your problem. For instance, when you were planning to capture Baby

Roo, one of the parts of your plan was that Kanga would have to be looking the other way. This is a good example of a constraint. It means that a plan in which Kanga was *not* looking the other way would not be an acceptable plan and would not work."

"And Kanga *did* look away," said Pooh proudly, "and our plan did work."

"Not completely, I don't think," said Piglet, remembering the taste of Roo's medicine and being a pig of a completely different color.

"So constraints are additional barriers or challenges that must be overcome to solve the problem," said The Stranger.

"And bees," said Pooh.

"And what happened next?" asked The Stranger.

Christopher Robin and Eeyore came strolling along together.

"I shouldn't be surprised if it hailed a good deal tomorrow," Eeyore was saying. "Blizzards and whatnot. Being fine today doesn't Mean Anything. It has no sig— what's that word? Well, it has none of that. It's just a small piece of weather."

"There's Pooh!" said Christopher Robin, who didn't much mind *what* it did tomorrow, as long as he was out in it. "Hallo, Pooh!"

"It's Christopher Robin!" said Piglet. "*He'll* know what to do."

They hurried up to him.

"Oh, Christopher Robin," began Pooh.

"And Eeyore," said Eeyore.

"Tigger and Roo are right up the Six Pine Trees, and they can't get down, and—"

"And I was just saying," put in Piglet, "that if only Christopher Robin—"

"*And* Eeyore—"

"If only you were here, then we could think of something to do."

Christopher Robin looked up at Tigger and Roo, and tried to think of something.

"Now it seems to me," said The Stranger, "that later on Eeyore does a Very Good Job of defining the problem and the constraints."

"Thank you," said Eeyore. "Probably just luck, that's what it must have been."

"No," said The Stranger. "It was well stated; you said—"

"*Getting Tigger down,*" said Eeyore, "and *Not hurting anybody.* Keep those two ideas in your head, Piglet, and you'll be all right."

"And there you have it," said The Stranger. "*Getting Tigger down* is the goal . . .*"

"And me too!" squealed Roo.

". . . and you too, Roo. And *Not hurting anybody.* A good example of a constraint, something that must be considered when you think of possible solutions. So we have created an accurate statement of what the problem was: Tigger and Roo are stuck up in a tree and we want to get them down without hurting anybody, and they can't climb down backward. The starting point is that Tigger and Roo are up in the tree, the desired goal is to get them down, and two constraints are that no one get hurt and that they can't climb down backward."

"Oh!" said Pooh suddenly, though he didn't quite know why. He was beginning to have a thought, but being a Bear of Very Little Brain, sometimes thoughts took quite a bit of waiting. Like playing his new game with sticks at the bridge. The time between when you dropped your sticks into the river and the time that you saw them come out under the bridge was the same kind of thing. So Pooh waited and waited for the idea, and kept saying "Oh!" over and over again.

"*Oh! O!*" Pooh exclaimed.

"What is it, Pooh?" asked Piglet.

"It's O. I just remembered when we were learning about management. There was an O in that too. It stood for organizing."

"So it did, Pooh," said The Stranger. "And that's a good way to remember this step too. Because we're doing much of the same thing here. We're taking a problem that we have selected—"

"Or that selected us," corrected Eeyore. "Forced itself upon us, that is. Even if we didn't want it."

"—and we're organizing it in a way that's easy to look at. We ask ourselves: Where are we now? and Where do we want to be? and also What else is important? Establishing the current situation, the goal we would like to achieve, and noticing any constraints, things in the way, as we examine the problem."

"So organizing is like getting ready!" said Piglet. "Like when you have invited Rabbit and his friends-and-relations over to tea, and you must run around and around getting everything that you need so that you'll be ready when they arrive, which is quite a lot as there are so many of them to get ready for."

"Why that's quite so, Piglet," said The Stranger. "Thank you for putting it so nicely."

"Did I say there were a lot of them?" added Piglet, just to make sure that he had let everyone know what it was like.

"Yes, you did. And when you organize a problem that you've selected—"

"Or that selected you," repeated Eeyore. "Forced, I'd call it."

"—it makes it easier," The Stranger continued, "to move to the next step—Learn, by Questioning All Parts of the Problem. But then, that is a subject for another day."

The Stranger stood up and began putting some additional wood onto the fire. Pooh moved back a little so that the sparks wouldn't singe his fur.

"Do you remember the rest of the story of how you were able to get Tigger down and not hurt anybody?" asked The Stranger. "The reason you were successful was that without realizing it, you were organizing the problem correctly and that made your solution a good one."

"Unless you were on the bottom," said Eeyore.

"What do you mean, Eeyore?" asked The Stranger.

And Eeyore recounted the rest of the tale—or tail, as he would have put it.

"I've got an idea!" cried Christopher Robin suddenly.

"Listen to this, Piglet," said Eeyore, "and then you'll know what we're trying to do."

"I'll take off my tunic and we'll each hold a corner, and then Roo and Tigger can jump into it, and it will be all soft and bouncy for them, and they won't hurt themselves."

"And that's where I said what the objective was," interrupted Eeyore.

"Yes," agreed The Stranger. "And then . . ."

When Roo understood what he had to do, he was wildly excited, and cried out: "Tigger, Tigger, we're going to jump! Look at me jumping, Tigger! Like flying, my jumping will be. Can Tiggers do it?" And he squeaked out: "I'm coming, Christopher Robin!" and he jumped—straight into the middle of the tunic. And he was going so fast that he bounced up again almost as high as where he was before—and went on bouncing and saying, "Oo!" for quite a long time—and then at last he stopped and said, "Oo, lovely!" And they put him on the ground.

"Come on, Tigger," he called out. "It's easy."

But Tigger was holding on to the branch and saying to himself: "It's all very well for Jumping Animals like Kangas, but it's quite different for Swimming Animals like Tiggers." And he thought of himself floating on his back down a river, or striking out from one island to another, and he felt that that was really the life for a Tigger.

"Come along," called Christopher Robin. "You'll be all right."

"Just wait a moment," said Tigger nervously. "Small piece of bark in my eye." And he moved slowly along his branch.

"Come on, it's easy!" squeaked Roo. And suddenly Tigger found how easy it was.

"Ow!" he shouted as the tree flew past him.

"Look out!" cried Christopher Robin to the others.

There was a crash, and a tearing noise, and a confused heap of everybody on the ground.

Christopher Robin and Pooh and Piglet picked themselves up first, and then they picked Tigger up, and underneath everybody else was Eeyore.

"Oh, Eeyore!" cried Christopher Robin. "Are you hurt?" And he felt him rather anxiously, and dusted him and helped him to stand up again.

Eeyore said nothing for a long time. And then he said: "Is Tigger there?"

Tigger was there, feeling Bouncy again already.

"Yes," said Christopher Robin. "Tigger's here."

"Well, just thank him for me," said Eeyore.

"I see," said The Stranger, laughing gently. "I hadn't remembered that part. I'm sorry, Eeyore. I hope you weren't hurt."

"It's all right," said Eeyore. "I only feel it when it's going to rain. Which should be any time now."

"There's one other thing I want to share with you," said The Stranger. "When we begin to work on a problem, this step is very important because how we Observe, Organize, and Define a problem often dictates how it is

solved. If we had observed the situation and had said the problem was not how to get Tigger and Roo down, but how to get Pooh and Piglet, and then Christopher Robin and Eeyore up into the Tallest Pine Tree, it would have been a completely different problem."

"A very Tall One," said Pooh.

"If we had said that the problem was to get Tigger and Roo down but left out the part about not hurting anybody—"

"That's the part I said," said Eeyore.

"—then the end of the adventure might have turned out quite differently," continued The Stranger. "So when we begin to solve problems, it is important to observe the problem carefully, to organize it by defining the starting point, the desired goal, and also to examine any constraints or difficulties that complicate the problem before taking another step."

"Especially if you are a Tigger Out On A Limb!" added Tigger.

"Well, I have enjoyed our talk and hope that you all had fun and learned about the second step in Problem Solving. Perhaps we can meet again if you'd like to learn about Learning."

The Stranger spent quite a few minutes using his long stick to move the burning embers apart and then spreading sand and dirt over them until the fire was completely out.

"That sounds twice as hard as just learning all by itself," said Pooh. "And learning by itself makes me hungry. Perhaps you could bring a Little Something to eat, just in case."

"That I shall," laughed The Stranger, who picked up his briefcase and walked off toward Owl's house, saying, "See you soon!" as he wandered out of sight.

Roo and Tigger bounded off together shouting, "Goodbye!" as they left for Kanga's house to play in the sand pit before supper.

"You did Very Well today, Piglet," said Pooh.

"Well, I *have* been to school, you know," said Piglet, making sure Pooh remembered.

"But now *I* have a problem!" said Pooh.

"That you're going to get soaked when it starts raining any minute now?" asked Eeyore.

"No, that it's too late for tea, but not quite time for supper. I know I won't be able to wait until supper, but then what do you call it if you have a little smackerel between?"

"That *is* a problem," said Piglet. "Well, you shall just have to come to my house. We'll think up a name for it while we have some. And you too, Eeyore."

"Thanks, no. I think I'll just stay here awhile and watch the rain. Perhaps I'll be struck by lightning."

So Pooh and Piglet wandered off toward Piglet's house, leaving Eeyore standing in the opening, eyeing the gath-

ering clouds. As they left, Eeyore could hear Pooh trying
out names of what you would call a smackerel that was too
late for tea and too early for supper.

"Tupper! No . . . uh . . . let's see . . . How about PasTea?
Or maybe . . ."

After a while Pooh decided that he would just call it
"Snack," and in that way he could use the same name if
he ran into the same problem with a smackerel that happened between breakfast and elevenses, or between lunch
and tea, or whatever. He spent the rest of the walk happily
humming a new hum, all about Problem Solving and what
The Stranger had been teaching them, and it went like
this:

> *Select the problem of the day,*
> *Finding one that's right to do,*
> *You can choose it either way,*
> *You pick it or it picks you.*
>
> *Observe it very carefully,*
> *"Where do I start? Where am I going?"*
> *And don't forget about the bee,*
> *"What's in the way of doing or knowing?"*

VI

IN WHICH Learning by Questioning Is
Talked About, a Horrible Heffalump
Is Trapped, and Pooh Finds He
Is a Very "Whys" Bear

"There he is!" Pooh and Piglet had spied The Stranger,
walking along the path that led to the open place where
they had met yesterday. "Hallo. Good Morning!"

"Good Morning, Pooh. Good Morning, Piglet. I'm
pleased to see you. Perhaps you'll walk with me the rest of
the way?"

They said they would, but didn't really, spending a
great deal of time hurrying ahead or dropping behind or
even wandering off to one side of the path or the other
when Something Interesting was noticed. After a short
while they reached the place and came upon Owl, perched
on a rock and looking around curiously. It wasn't that he
was being curious and looking around as much as it was
that when he looked around he was able to turn his head
completely in circles, and it was quite curious, unless you
too could turn your head that way.

"Hallo, Owl!" said Pooh.

"Hallo, Pooh," said Owl.

"Good Morning, Owl," said The Stranger. "Have you seen Tigger and Roo? And Eeyore? I thought they were going to join us this morning."

"They were here," replied Owl, "but they said something about going past Christopher Robin's house to play on the river where the Big Stones and Rox are."

"Well, perhaps they'll be back in a little bit, just in time for lunch," said The Stranger, lifting his picnic basket and placing it on a stump nearby.

Pooh looked longingly at the basket. "I hope they won't be too long."

"Let us get started anyway," said The Stranger, "and they can join in when they return. Now—"

"Why?" asked Pooh, really wanting to know how long they would have to wait.

"Because I think it would be better to get started, as we have a great deal to talk about," explained The Stranger.

"Why?" repeated Pooh.

"Well, because today we'll be talking about the third step in Problem Solving: Learn by Questioning. And there's a lot to it," said The Stranger.

"Why?" said Pooh and Piglet together, Piglet having caught on and wanting to be part of the conversation, as he was sure it was beginning to go Somewhere.

The Stranger looked back and forth between Pooh and

Piglet. "Because after we have Selected a Problem, or have had one selected for us, as I'm sure Eeyore would have pointed out if he were here; and after we have Observed, Organized, and Defined a problem by stating accurately what the problem is, where we're starting from, what our goal is, and if there is anything else we should consider; it is helpful to next find out as much as we can about it."

"Why?" This time Owl joined in with Pooh and Piglet.

"I can see you've gotten ahead of me," laughed The Stranger. Pooh looked over his shoulder thinking that if they had gotten ahead of The Stranger, then surely he would be behind them, but he saw only the heather and gorse bushes by the edge of the clearing.

"That's a Very Good Question," continued The Stranger. "One of the best, in fact. The reason why we ask questions during this part of the process is to confirm the facts of the problem or to verify some of what is already known. We might want to ask questions to find out things that we don't know or to fill in gaps in what we *do* know. We also ask questions to gauge the relative importance of different elements."

"What are 'elements'?" Pooh whispered to Piglet.

"I think those are a special kind of Heffalump," Piglet answered. "They are gray and have long tusks."

"Larger and fiercer than your normal Heffalump," added Owl, "and primarily found in wetter areas with greater precipitation."

"Why?" asked Pooh, again, proud of his determination to get to the Bottom of Things.

"Because the wetter conditions provide an increase in Floral and Faunal diversity which then engenders a greater environmental—"

"No. Why do we want to know those things?" said Pooh, having understood only the first couple of words that Owl had said anyway, and beginning to look around for Tigger and Roo and Eeyore, as all this talk was making him quite hungry.

"For different reasons," replied The Stranger. "Confirming facts or verifying what we already know is done to make sure that when we stated the problem, we stated it correctly. Finding out things we don't know, or filling in gaps in what we *do* know, helps us to understand the nature of the problem and what the problem is about. Finally, asking questions to gauge the relative importance of different ele . . . um . . . parts of the problem helps direct our attention to the parts that are most responsible for it being a problem in the first place."

"The problem parts!" squeaked Piglet.

"Just so," said The Stranger. "Piglet, perhaps you can tell us about the time you met a Heffalump? If I remember, that's a good example of just what we're talking about."

And so Piglet stood up, just as he had seen Christopher Robin do in school when reciting his work, and began his story. "Well, one day Pooh said . . ."

"Piglet, I have decided something."

"What have you decided, Pooh?"

"I have decided to catch a Heffalump."

Pooh nodded his head several times as he said this, and waited for Piglet to say "How?" or "Pooh, you couldn't!" or something helpful of that sort, but Piglet said nothing. The fact was Piglet was wishing that *he* had thought about it first.

"I shall do it," said Pooh, after waiting a little longer, "by means of a trap. And it must be a Cunning Trap, so you will have to help me, Piglet."

"Pooh," said Piglet, feeling quite happy again now, "I will." And then he said, "How shall we do it?" and Pooh said, "That's just it. How?" And then they sat down together to think it out.

Pooh's first idea was that they should dig a Very Deep Pit, and then the Heffalump would come along and fall into the Pit, and—

"Why?" said Piglet.

"Why what?" said Pooh.

"Why would he fall in?"

Pooh rubbed his nose with his paw, and said that the Heffalump might be walking along, humming a little song, and looking up at the sky, wondering if it would rain, so he wouldn't see the Very Deep Pit until he was half-way down, when it would be too late.

Piglet said that this was a very good Trap, but supposing it were raining already?

Pooh rubbed his nose again, and said that he hadn't thought of that. And then he brightened up, and said that, if it were raining already, the Heffalump would be looking at the sky wondering if it would *clear up,* and so he wouldn't see the Very Deep Pit until he was half-way down. . . . When it would be too late.

Piglet said that, now that this point had been explained, he thought it was a Cunning Trap.

"So you see," said The Stranger, "Piglet was doing a good job of asking questions." Piglet stopped squirming around where he was sitting and beamed proudly at the others. "When Pooh decided that he would catch a Heffalump, that was the selection of the problem to be solved. And Pooh's declaration that he would catch one by using a Cunning Trap was a result of his observations on the nature of Heffalumps, and his organization and definition of the problem of catching Heffalumps. Piglet's questions about why the Heffalump would fall in the trap and also about what might happen if it were raining already are also good questions that serve to help them examine the problem and fill in their understanding of Heffalumps and Cunning Traps."

"I learned that at school," squeaked Piglet.

"Did you now?" replied The Stranger. "Tell me about your schooling."

"Christopher Robin took me. He put me in his pocket," Piglet said, pausing to make sure that everyone was listening. "School was mostly about questions, as a matter of fact."

"Education often utilizes an interrogatory or Socratic forum for dispensation or transference of intellectual or pragmatic erudition," said Owl.

Pooh understood the words "education," as it was something he didn't have; "often," as it was how frequently he became hungry, like right now; and "or" and "of"; but the rest of what Owl said only served to confuzzle him. And he was much more easily confuzzled when he was hungry, he told himself. He looked around one more time, hoping that Tigger and Roo and Eeyore might just now be returning.

"Yes," Piglet agreed with Owl, although he hadn't really understood any more of what Owl had said than Pooh. "And if most of school was about questions, the rest of it was all filled up with answers."

The Stranger noticed Pooh's attention elsewhere, and guessed what it was that had him shifting and fidgeting and looking around. "Before we go on, I think we should have a bite to eat. I was going to wait for the others, but they'll be along shortly, no doubt, and there's plenty, so let's start without them."

Pooh was overjoyed and proved extremely helpful to The Stranger, unloading his basket and making sure exactly what everything was as he removed it from the hamper.

"One of the interesting things about questions," continued The Stranger as they all enjoyed their lunch, "is that sometimes the answers to questions require more questions to be asked."

"Like when you're having honey and condensed milk," said Pooh stickily, making sure that the honey that The Stranger had brought was really honey all the way to the bottom, and not honey-colored cheese of the kind his uncle had mentioned, "and it doesn't come out right and you have to have a little more milk to even out the honey and then a little more honey because now you've not got enough."

"Exactly," continued The Stranger. "Finding out all you can about a problem by asking questions helps you to understand all aspects of the problem and will be important when we talk about visualizing potential solutions. Now, let's see . . . how did the story continue?"

"I know, I know!" squealed Piglet, jumping up and down, finally settling down enough to continue. "It was right after I had said that it seemed a Cunning Trap."

Pooh was very proud when he heard this, and he felt that the Heffalump was as good as caught already, but there was just one other thing which had to be thought about, and it was this. *Where should they dig the Very Deep Pit?*

Piglet said that the best place would be somewhere where a Heffalump was, just before he fell into it, only about a foot farther on.

"But then he would see us digging it," said Pooh.

"Not if he was looking at the sky."

"He would Suspect," said Pooh, "if he happened to look down." He thought for a long time and then added sadly, "It isn't as easy as I thought. I suppose that's why Heffalumps hardly *ever* get caught."

"That must be it," said Piglet.

They sighed and got up; and when they had taken a few gorse prickles out of themselves they sat down again; and all the time Pooh was saying to himself, "If only I could *think* of something!" For he felt sure that a Very Clever Brain could catch a Heffalump if only he knew the right way to go about it.

"Suppose," he said to Piglet, "*you* wanted to catch *me*, how would you do it?"

"Well," said Piglet, "I should do it like this. I should make a Trap, and I should put a Jar of Honey in the Trap, and you would smell it, and you would go in after it, and—"

"And I would go in after it," said Pooh excitedly, "only very carefully so as not to hurt myself, and I would get to the Jar of Honey, and I should lick round the edges first of all, pretending that there wasn't any more, you know, and then I should walk away and think about it a little, and then I should come back and start licking in the middle of the jar, and then—"

"Yes, well never mind about that. There you would be, and there I should catch you. Now the first thing to think of is, What do Heffalumps like? I should think acorns, shouldn't you? We'll get a lot of—I say, wake up, Pooh!"

Pooh, who had gone into a happy dream, woke up with a start, thinking that Piglet was talking to him, and not just retelling part of the story.

"So you see," said The Stranger, "both Pooh and Piglet are asking questions to find out more about how they should go about trapping the Heffalump."

"How many questions are there?" asked Pooh.

"That is an impertinent question, Pooh," said Owl. "You should have been paying more attention."

"Now wait a moment, Owl," said The Stranger. "There are no bad questions. Or foolish ones, or even ones that are too simple or silly. This is Very Important. *Any* question must be regarded seriously no matter how basic or silly. Often, the simplest questions are the best ones because they address issues that are most fundamental or meaningful to a particular problem."

That kind of bear, thought Pooh.

"Let me give you an example," continued The Stranger. "Let us say you are a businessman."

"You are a businessman," repeated Pooh and Piglet. Owl stared at them.

"You might think it silly to ask yourself 'What business am I in?' as you would think that you already must know exactly what business it is you are in. You might say 'That's silly! I am in the book-publishing business' or 'I am in the insurance business' or whatever it was that you did. But if you question yourself and reflect more carefully on exactly what it is you do, and for whom, and how it is you really accomplish your work, you may find surprising answers.

"You may *think* you're in the book-publishing business, but really you are in the information-management business, which means you may be able to make other products as well: databases, audiotapes, multimedia CD-ROMs, or computer disks. Or if you're in insurance, you may realize that you're really in the business of helping people plan their finances, investing, and estate planning."

"If I were to plan an estate," added Piglet, "it would be quite grand, with lots of rooms and a large pool in the backyard."

"And a library and study," said Owl.

"And *two* larders!" said Pooh.

"So by asking questions," continued The Stranger, "even seemingly simple or basic ones, you can learn a great deal about whatever it is you are examining. The other thing about questions is that there are really only six different kinds. Do you know the five W's?"

"Of course," said Owl, "they were a world famous family of high-wire tightrope acrobats from many years ago. I think their name was Wallenda."

"Actually," said The Stranger, "I was thinking of the five 'W' questions: Why? What? Where? When? and Who?, which, along with How?, make up the six different kinds of questions."

"Who?" said Owl.

"Exactly," said The Stranger. "Using these six different kinds of questions on the different parts of our problem, we can easily generate a whole range of questions that, when we find the answers, will help us to understand the problem more fully."

"Who? What? When? Why? How? Where?" squeaked Piglet, trying out the six different kinds of questions and liking the way they sounded.

"You've got them all," said The Stranger, "but it is important that you use them in the right order too."

"There's an order to them?" asked Pooh, thinking that this must be Important, and trying his best to get ready to remember.

"Yes," said The Stranger, "the order is Very Important.

The first question you ask about any problem you are trying to solve is Why solve this problem? The reason that you ask this question first is that if you can't find a good reason, maybe you don't need to solve this problem at all!"

"That's the kind of problem I like," said Pooh.

"The next question to ask," continued The Stranger, "is What? as in, What exactly is the problem I'm trying to solve? In the last step, when we were to Observe, Organize, and Define the problem, we determined the current situation, the desired goal, and any constraints. Here, we ask ourselves What? to focus on the specific nature of the problem. If we are able to answer this question, it will help us to understand better and develop better solutions. But that's not all. For What? and all the following questions, when we find answers, we then also ask Why? and the Why? makes us examine the answers we get even more closely."

"So the precise order," said Owl, "is Why? and then: What? Why? Where? Why? When? Why? Who? Why? and How? Why?"

"Well done, Owl," said The Stranger.

Pooh felt he must have missed something. He could remember the five W's, and even the How, but now there were a lot of extra Whys all over the place, and it was making him hungry. "So . . . it's a good idea . . . to ask . . . Why? a lot?"

"Yes, indeed. When you ask Why? after answering the

other W questions, you are trying to find the reasons behind the answers and to understand the problem better. Here, let's use a quick example. Say . . . uh, er, suppose you were—"

"Hungry!" said Pooh.

"All right," said The Stranger. "The problem is that you are hungry. The first question we said you should ask is Why? as in Why should you solve this problem?"

"Why, because I'd much rather be full," said Pooh.

"The second question," continued The Stranger, "is What?, perhaps What are you hungry for?"

"Honey!" said Pooh, dreamily.

"And after we get an answer to one of our W questions, we then ask Why? Pooh, why are you hungry for honey?"

"Well," said Pooh slowly, "I . . . think . . . it's . . . um. I don't know why. Perhaps some cake would be nice too, or even some condensed milk."

"So we know now," said The Stranger, "that while you are hungry for honey, you could also be happy with cake or condensed milk. So we learned of two other ways to solve the problem that you are hungry."

Pooh's tummy began to rumble. "Does solving problems always make you so hungry?"

"Not always," said The Stranger. "So the order of the questions is meant to approach the problem's most important aspects first." The Stranger took a stick and wrote in the dirt so that all could see, and this is what he wrote:

WHY SHOULD THIS PROBLEM BE SOLVED?

WHAT IS THE PROBLEM?	WHY IS IT A PROBLEM?
WHERE DOES THE PROBLEM OCCUR?	WHY DOES IT OCCUR THERE?
WHEN DOES THE PROBLEM OCCUR?	WHY DOES IT OCCUR THEN?
WHO IS INVOLVED WITH THE PROBLEM?	WHY ARE THEY INVOLVED?
HOW DOES THE PROBLEM ARISE?	WHY DOES IT ARISE IN THAT WAY?

"But you still haven't explained why," said Piglet.

"Why what?" said The Stranger.

"Why *that* particular order?"

"You're right, Piglet," said The Stranger. "I'm sorry. The reason we use that particular order is that the questions are arranged to find out about things that are most easily or least expensively changed first. Changing *where* something is done is generally less of an undertaking, less difficult or costly, than changing *how* something is done. So if we can solve our problem based on an earlier question, it often is less troublesome or costly to correct."

"I always have trouble with the Hows," said Pooh.

"In our story," said The Stranger, "Pooh asks himself *Where* should he dig the Very Deep Pit and also asks Piglet *How* he would go about catching Pooh. Both are good examples of questions that will help them to solve their problem about catching Heffalumps."

"But not much help once you've got one," added Pooh.

"Well, let's see," said The Stranger, "what was the rest of the story?"

"Honey," said Piglet to himself in a thoughtful way, as if it were now settled. "*I'll* dig the pit, while *you* go and get the honey."

"Very well," said Pooh, and he stumped off.

As soon as he got home, he went to the larder; and he stood on a chair, and took down a very large jar of honey from the top shelf. It had HUNNY written on it,

but, just to make sure, he took off the paper cover and looked at it, and it *looked* just like honey. "But you never can tell," said Pooh. . . . So he put his tongue in, and took a large lick. "Yes," he said, "it is. No doubt about that. . . ." And he gave a deep sigh. "I *was* right. It *is* honey, right the way down."

Having made certain of this, he took the jar back to

Piglet, and Piglet looked up from the bottom of his Very Deep Pit, and said, "Got it?" and Pooh said, "Yes, but it isn't quite a full jar," and he threw it down to Piglet, and Piglet said, "No, it isn't! Is that all you've got left?" and Pooh said, "Yes."

"Well, good night, Pooh," said Piglet, when they had got to Pooh's house. "And we meet at six o'clock to-morrow morning by the Pine Trees, and see how many Heffalumps we've got in our Trap."

"Good night!"

By and by Piglet woke up. As soon as he woke he said to himself, "Oh!" Then he said bravely, "Yes," and then, still more bravely, "Quite so." But he didn't feel very brave, for the word which was really jiggeting about in his brain was "Heffalumps."

What was a Heffalump like?

Was it Fierce?

Did it come when you whistled? And *how* did it come?

Was it Fond of Pigs at all?

If it was Fond of Pigs, did it make any difference *what sort of Pig?*

Supposing it was Fierce with Pigs, would it make any difference *if the Pig had a grandfather called TRESPASS-ERS WILLIAM?*

He didn't know the answer to any of these questions . . . and he was going to see his first Heffalump in about an hour from now!

Of course Pooh would be with him, and it was much more Friendly with two. But suppose Heffalumps were Very Fierce with Pigs *and* Bears? Wouldn't it be better to pretend that he had a headache, and couldn't go up to the Six Pine Trees this morning? . . . What should he do?

And then he had a Clever Idea. He would go up very quietly to the Six Pine Trees now, peep very cautiously into the Trap, and see if there *was* a Heffalump there. And if there was, he would go back to bed, and if there wasn't, he wouldn't.

So off he went. At first he thought that there wouldn't be a Heffalump in the Trap, and then he thought that there would, and as he got nearer he was *sure* that there would, because he could hear it heffalumping about, . . . like anything.

"Oh, dear, oh, dear, oh, dear!" said Piglet to himself. And he wanted to run away. But somehow, having got so near, he felt that he must just see what a Heffalump was like. So he crept to the side of the Trap and looked in. . . .

"So we see," interrupted The Stranger, just when the story was getting interesting, "Piglet does a very fine job of making up questions about the Heffalump. And even devises a Clever Plan to find out the answers to them, being Very Brave at the same time."

"I think if I had gotten some of the answers," said Piglet, "I wouldn't have gone to the Very Deep Pit at all."

"And that's a good point too," said The Stranger. "Sometimes the answers to your questions about a problem may require that you go back a step and revise the statement of the problem or the goal or even add additional constraints. Often it can be helpful to go back and forth between the different steps of the Problem-Solving Method to make sure that your assumptions still hold. It's called iterating, meaning doing something over and over again."

Pooh hadn't quite been paying attention, except for the last part, when he thought The Stranger had said, "We should be eating . . . over and over again," which made quite a lot of sense to him just then. A Large Commotion began in the bushes to one side of the clearing, and out bounced Tigger, with Roo clutching tightly to his back.

"Whee!" squeaked Roo.

"Ow!" howled Tigger, stopping his bouncing just long enough to pick some prickles out of his fur.

"Good morning, Tigger! Good morning, Roo!" said The Stranger. "You're just in time for lunch. We've been learning about the third step in Problem Solving, Learning by Asking Questions."

"Like 'When would you like your honey, now or later?' and 'How would you like to pass the condensed milk, please?'" said Pooh.

"Well, not exactly like that," said The Stranger, "but I can see you're trying to solve your problem of being hungry, so let me help." He passed Pooh a jar of honey that he had brought along and began serving the rest of the lunch to the others. "Now, if you remember, Piglet had gone to the Heffalump Trap and looked in. . . ."

And all the time Winnie-the-Pooh had been trying to get the honey-jar off his head. The more he shook it, the more tightly it stuck. *"Bother!"* he said, inside the jar, and *"Oh, help!"* and, mostly *"Ow!"* And he tried bumping it against things, but as he couldn't see what he was bumping it against, it didn't help him; and he tried to climb out of the Trap, but as he could see nothing but jar, and not much of that, he couldn't find his way. So at last he lifted up his head, jar and all, and made a loud, roaring noise of Sadness and Despair . . . and it was at that moment that Piglet looked down.

"Help, help!" cried Piglet, "a Heffalump, a Horrible Heffalump!" and he scampered off as hard as he could, still crying out, "Help, help, a Herrible Hoffalump! Hoff, Hoff, a Hellible Horralump! Holl, Holl a Hoffable Hellerump!" And he didn't stop crying and scampering until he got to Christopher Robin's house.

"Whatever's the matter, Piglet?" said Christopher Robin, who was just getting up.

"Heff," said Piglet, breathing so hard that he could hardly speak, "a Hell—a Heff—a Heffalump."

"Where?"

"Up there," said Piglet, waving his paw.

"What did it look like?"

"Like—like—It had the biggest head you ever saw, Christopher Robin. A great enormous thing, like—like nothing. A huge big—well, like a—I don't know—like an enormous big nothing. Like a jar."

"Well," said Christopher Robin, putting on his shoes, "I shall go and look at it. Come on."

Piglet wasn't afraid if he had Christopher Robin with him, so off they went. . . .

"I can hear it, can't you?" said Piglet anxiously, as they got near.

"I can hear *something*," said Christopher Robin. It was Pooh bumping his head against a tree-root he had found.

"There!" said Piglet. "Isn't it *awful?*" And he held on tight to Christopher Robin's hand.

Suddenly, Christopher Robin began to laugh . . . and he laughed . . . and he laughed . . . and he laughed.

"I think that I am getting a headache," said Piglet, remembering how foolish he had felt when the Horrible Heffalump turned out to be Pooh.

"Don't feel badly, Piglet," said The Stranger. "It must have been very easy to mistake Pooh for a Horrible Heffalump, especially since he was wearing a jar on his head and howling in the bottom of a Heffalump Trap."

"Although everyone knows," said Owl, "that Heffalumps are migratory and herbivorous and aren't usually found in this wood except in the spring."

Pooh didn't know this, and so tried to change the subject, saying, "Christopher Robin was Asking Important Questions in the story, wasn't he?"

"Yes," said The Stranger. "When Piglet presented him with the problem of having found a Heffalump . . ."

"Or what *looked* like a Heffalump," said Piglet.

". . . Christopher Robin immediately asked Where? and What? to find out more about it. So you see, asking questions is a very good way to find things out, confirm facts, and assess whatever problem you are facing. The six different kinds of questions will help you to do this: Why? What? Where? When? Who? and How? Remember too that the order of the questions is Important, and that when we find an answer to the questions, we then ask Why? so that we can try to understand the reasons behind the answers. When we've finished asking questions, we should know a great deal more than when we started, and we should begin to see ways we might solve the problem. And that will be our next step—Visualize Possible Solutions, Select One, and Refine It.

"Finally, remember: the questions you ask about the problem may give you answers that make you revise your statement of the problem, its goals, or the addition of constraints."

"Which are sometimes bees," stated Pooh.

"Oh, Bear!" said The Stranger fondly.

VII
IN WHICH Visualizing Possible Solutions Is Practiced, a Briefcase Is Rescued, and Pooh Adds Two Verses

Pooh and Piglet were walking in the Forest, when they came upon The Stranger standing at the edge of a Very Deep Pit with his hands on his hips and staring down at the bottom of it.

"Hallo!" said Pooh and Piglet at once.

"What are you doing?" asked Pooh.

"I am trying to Visualize Possible Solutions," said The Stranger.

"I don't see anything," said Pooh, looking down into the pit just to make sure.

"I mean I am trying to think of solutions to solve a small problem that I have," said The Stranger. "I was walking along this path, when I stumbled and fell, and it seems I have dropped my briefcase into this Very Deep Pit that someone has left here."

"A problem!" squealed Piglet. "Oh! Oh! A real problem."

Pooh quickly tried to think of the five steps in the Problem-Solving Method that The Stranger had told him about. He wanted very much to be Helpful. "Have you . . . uh . . . Observed the Problem?"

The Stranger stopped staring into the blackness at the bottom of the Pit and saw that Pooh was trying out the Problem Solving that he had been learning about. "Very good, Pooh. Why, yes, and let me tell you what I have learned so far and perhaps you can help me solve it now that you are here. As I said, I was walking along and tripped and fell, and my briefcase fell into the Pit. Once this problem selected me, as Eeyore no doubt would have put it, I Observed that I am at the top of the Pit, that I would like to have my briefcase back, and that there is a Very Large Drop from here to the bottom of the Pit that is keeping me from getting my briefcase easily."

"If you were a Jagular, it wouldn't be very hard at all," said Piglet. "Jagulars are very good droppers."

"So now we ask questions?" asked Pooh. Pooh tried to remember the correct order. "Why! Yes, that's it, Why?"

"Good," said The Stranger. "Because I would like to have my briefcase back, as I have lots of important things in there."

Pooh knew the next question should be a What? question.

"What . . . did you have in the briefcase?" asked Pooh.

"Pooh, I'm glad you remembered that the next thing to ask was a What? question, but I think we should rather ask, What is the nature of the problem? or What is keeping us from getting the briefcase?"

"What *is* keeping us from getting the briefcase?" said Pooh.

"Well," said The Stranger, "the Pit is Very Deep, and I cannot see the briefcase, and even if I could, I don't think I could reach to the bottom and get it."

Pooh was ready. "Why?" he asked.

"Why, because the Pit is so deep or my arms are so short, or perhaps both," said The Stranger.

Pooh thought of asking a Where? but he was sure the answer was Here! and he was about to ask a When? or a

Who? but was just as sure it was Now! and Us! so he thought hard and asked a How? "How exactly did you fall?"

"I was walking down this path," said The Stranger, "and I guess I was looking at the flowers there, when all of a sudden I tripped, and fell forward about here."

"And the briefcase was gone?" asked Piglet.

"Yes, quite," said The Stranger. "And then I got up and looked around and realized I had a problem. I began to go through the Problem-Solving Method, as we have done now, and was at just this point when you walked up. Which is good, in a way, as I did want to spend some time with you talking about the very next step in the process— Visualize Possible Solutions, Select One, and Refine It. So let's sit down and see if we can learn about this step and solve this problem at the same time. If we do, we will have two rewards—if we *do* solve it, of course."

"I still think it is important to know *What* is in the briefcase," said Pooh.

"If you think it will help," said The Stranger, "I had all of my notes for the book I am writing, my laptop computer, and some other papers and things."

Pooh was disappointed that The Stranger didn't have anything Good to Eat in his briefcase. "Are you sure that's all you had?" he asked, and The Stranger nodded.

"Now," said The Stranger, "we have reviewed the first three steps of our Problem-Solving Method. The next, Visualizing Possible Solutions, is the one I find the most fun. We'll see how creativity and experience are helpful in thinking up solutions, how you can take different approaches depending on the problem, and even some useful techniques that will help you come up with more solutions when you can't think of any. Of course, once we have thought of some solutions, we'll need to review them and pick the best one, and then spend a little more time refining our best solution to improve its chance of success."

"That sounds like a lot of work to do," said Pooh, ". . . before lunch."

"Then we should begin right away," said The Stranger. "And the place to begin is with creativity and experience. Both of these are very useful when it comes to solving problems. And, while some people might say that creativity is a thing that you either have or you don't have, I've found that it really is a way of being, of looking at things without judging them first, and that it can be learned and improved. And experience is just the remembering of having solved other problems in the past, and not forgetting the things that worked, and also the things that didn't. Let me explain. Do you remember that Blusterous Day when Owl's house came crashing down with both you and Owl inside?"

"Well!" said Owl. "This is a nice state of things!"

"What are we going to do, Pooh? Can you think of anything?" asked Piglet. . . .

Owl coughed in an unadmiring sort of way, and said that . . . they could now give their minds to the Problem of Escape.

"Because," said Owl, "we can't go out by what used to be the front door. Something's fallen on it."

"But how else *can* you go out?" asked Piglet anxiously.

"That is the Problem, Piglet, to which I am asking Pooh to give his mind."

Pooh sat on the floor which had once been a wall, and gazed up at the ceiling which had once been another wall, with a front door in it which had once been a front door, and tried to give his mind to it.

"Could you fly up to the letter-box with Piglet on your back?" he asked.

"No," said Piglet quickly. "He couldn't."

Owl explained about the Necessary Dorsal Muscles. He had explained this to Pooh and Christopher Robin once before, and had been waiting ever since for a chance to do it again, because it is a thing which you can easily explain twice before anybody knows what you are talking about.

"Because you see, Owl, if we could get Piglet into the letter-box, he might squeeze through the place where the letters come, and climb down the tree and run for help."

Piglet said hurriedly that he had been getting bigger lately, and couldn't *possibly*, much as he would like to, and Owl said that he had had his letter-box made bigger lately in case he got bigger letters, so perhaps Piglet *might*, and Piglet said, "But you said the Necessary you-know-whats *wouldn't*," and Owl said, "No, they *won't*, so it's no good thinking about it," and Piglet said, "Then we'd better think of something else," and began to at once.

But Pooh's mind had gone back to the day when he had saved Piglet from the flood, and everybody had admired him so much; and as that didn't often happen he thought he would like it to happen again. And suddenly, just as it had come before, an idea came to him.

"Owl," said Pooh, "I have thought of something."

"Astute and Helpful Bear," said Owl.

Pooh looked proud at being called a stout and helpful bear, and said modestly that he just happened to think of it. You tied a piece of string to Piglet, and you flew up to the letter-box with the other end in your beak, and you pushed it through the wire and brought it down to the floor, and you and Pooh pulled hard at this end, and Piglet went slowly up at the other end. And there you were.

"And there Piglet is," said Owl. "If the string doesn't break."

"Supposing it does?" asked Piglet, wanting to know.

"Then we try another piece of string."

This was not very comforting to Piglet, because however many pieces of string they tried pulling up with, it would always be the same him coming down; but still, it did seem the only thing to do. So with one last look back in his mind at all the happy hours he had spent in the Forest *not* being pulled up to the ceiling by a piece of string, Piglet nodded bravely at Pooh and said that it was a Very Clever pup-pup-pup Clever pup-pup Plan.

"So you see, Pooh," said The Stranger, "you were being creative when you thought of having Owl fly up to the letter-box with Piglet on his back."

"But that's not what we ended up doing," Piglet pointed out.

"That's true," said The Stranger. "But part of the way creativity helps is that one idea reminds you of another, which lets you make up many possible solutions to your problem. From these, you can choose the best one. The more solutions you have to choose from, the greater your chance of success."

"But what about *this* problem?" said Piglet.

"We could send Piglet into the Pit and have him find the briefcase and throw it up to us," said Pooh.

"That's a terrible idea!" squeaked Piglet.

"Now, wait a moment, Piglet," said The Stranger. "One of the things about creativity is that it is very fragile, and nothing stops creativity more surely than saying an idea won't work or is bad."

"I just meant . . . uh, that . . ." stammered Piglet, "that the Pit is Very Deep, and I don't know how you would send me in, and even after you did, if I *were* to find the briefcase, I don't know if I could throw it up to you, and even after that I would still be in the Very Deep Pit and would feel a lot like the briefcase does now, I suppose, not knowing how or if it will get out."

"Those are all very good points," said The Stranger, "and when we select ideas later and begin to refine them, we shall take that into account, but while we are thinking of ideas it is important not to judge them ahead of time or pretty soon no one will have any."

"We should send Pooh into the Pit and have *him* find the briefcase and throw it up to us!" shouted Piglet.

"Yes!" said Pooh, thinking about how he could check to make sure that everything in the briefcase was all right before rescuing it, and that The Stranger might have forgotten about a little smackerel he had packed inside, and not thinking at all about how he might get out.

"So creativity helps us Visualize Possible Solutions by allowing us to think up many possible solutions to choose from, and it is important that we remember that no criticizing of ideas is allowed. Any idea serves by either being one of many, or by making you think of another idea that you wouldn't have thought of if you hadn't heard the first idea. Now, experience helps by letting you use other similar problems that you have heard about or have solved in the past. It can also help by giving you an appreciation of those solutions that work and those that don't based on your own or someone else's previous attempts to solve a similar problem."

"Just as in Owl's house, when Pooh was remembering how he had saved me from the flood," said Piglet.

"That's right," said The Stranger. "Pooh remembered solving a difficult problem in the past, and it gave him confidence to think of a solution when you were stuck in Owl's house."

"Or when Tigger and Roo were stuck up in a tree and I thought of a way to rescue them," said Piglet, as he reminded them exactly how it had been:

"I thought," said Piglet earnestly, "that if Eeyore stood at the bottom of the tree, and if Pooh stood on Eeyore's back, and if I stood on Pooh's shoulders—"

"And if Eeyore's back snapped suddenly, then we could all laugh. Ha ha! Amusing in a quiet way," said Eeyore, "but not really helpful."

"Well," said Piglet meekly, "I thought—"

"Would it break your back, Eeyore?" asked Pooh, very much surprised.

"That's what would be so interesting, Pooh. Not being quite sure till afterwards."

Pooh said "Oh!" and they all began to think again.

"But we didn't use that idea to rescue Tigger and Roo," said Piglet sadly, "though I really think it might have worked."

"But every idea is important," said The Stranger, "because it leads to the next idea even if it doesn't solve the problem itself."

"So what do we do for this problem?" asked Pooh.

"What do you think?" said The Stranger.

"Well," said Pooh, beginning to think very hard about the briefcase at the bottom of the Pit. "We could go and get Owl, and have him fly down into the Pit, find the briefcase, and pick it up and fly out with it."

"Very Good, Pooh!" said The Stranger.

"Do you really think it will work?" asked Pooh.

"Perhaps," said The Stranger, "but what is important is that we are generating more ideas, and remember, the more ideas we have to choose from, the better our chance of finding a successful one."

"Perhaps we should do what we did before," said Piglet.

"What do you mean?" asked The Stranger.

"String Theory," said Piglet, knowing once he said it that it sounded Familiar and Good.

"You mean Cosmic String Theory?" asked The Stranger.

"No, we'll call Owl and have him take a bit of string down into the Pit in his beak and put it around the handle and bring it back up to us, just as we did at Owl's house. Then we can pull the briefcase up from here."

"That's very good, Piglet," said The Stranger. "That's a very good use of your experience too." And Piglet felt very proud.

"But before we choose one solution," said The Stranger, "let's talk a little bit about how different approaches are useful for different problems. There are many different approaches you can use to come up with potential solutions to problems. A numerical approach, or using numbers, might be good for problems that deal with quantities of things. Graphical approaches can be useful for problems where drawings or pictures make solving the problem easier, like using maps to find your way. Analogy can be a powerful tool for developing solutions. This is where you compare the problem for which you need a solution with a similar process or event whose solution you know. That then suggests a possible solution for *your* problem. An intuitive approach to a problem would use your common sense to reason a solution for a particular problem."

"How do you know which one to use?" asked Pooh.

"Often, the problem itself tells you," said The Stranger.

"I don't hear anything," said Pooh, leaning over the edge of the Pit and listening carefully.

"Perhaps I should have said that your experience with other problems," said The Stranger, "and common sense should help you."

"But with all the problems there are," said Pooh, "common sense doesn't seem very *common*."

"That's a good point," said The Stranger. "We'll help you to learn how to solve problems, so you can have uncommon common sense."

"I'd like that."

"But you can see that if your problem was finding your way, a numerical approach would be hard to apply and certainly wouldn't give you many possible solutions to choose from. That's another way to know whether you have the right approach—whether it offers good possible solutions or many of them."

"But what if you can't think of anything?" asked Piglet.

"In that case," said The Stranger, "there *are* some ways to generate more ideas and they're fun to do since they *are* a sort of game."

"Oh, oh!" said Piglet, jumping up and down and running around and almost falling in the Very Deep Pit. "Teach me! I want to play!"

"Actually, Piglet, I'm sure you already know," said The Stranger. "Remember before, when you said that if you were a Jagular you could jump right into the Pit because they are very good droppers?"

"Yes, but I was just pretending," said Piglet.

"Well, this part of Problem Solving is about pretending," said The Stranger. "What we do to create more ideas for possible solutions is to pretend that one part of the problem is different than it really is. Let me show you." And The Stranger took a stick, because his laptop computer was inside the briefcase at the bottom of the Pit, and wrote in the dirt:

Make it bigger
Make it smaller
Add something
Take something away
Exchange two parts
Remove something
Replace something with something else
Combine two elements
Free association

"The way we play this game is to take the problem we have," continued The Stranger, "and pretend that it is a little bit different. For instance, let's pretend that the briefcase is bigger. Much bigger. Bigger than a house!"

"But then you'd need a crane to get it out of the Pit!" said Pooh, imagining how big such a briefcase must be.

"Perfect!" shouted The Stranger. "That's exactly how to play! So one way to get the briefcase out would be to use a crane. Now since our briefcase is not really as large as a house, the crane *we* would need could be very much smaller. But without playing the game, we might not have thought of trying a crane at all."

"How exactly does that help us?" asked Pooh.

"What happens," said The Stranger, "is that when we change the problem in some way by making part of it larger or smaller, or doing any of the things we mentioned, it helps us to see the problem in a new light, to examine the relationship of the different parts of the problem to one another in a new way. And often that can lead to new ideas about how we might go about solving it."

"Let's keep playing," squeaked Piglet, and so they did. They imagined they were smaller, as small as Small, and could walk right down the side of the Pit. They imagined adding water to the Pit and floating the briefcase out. They imagined the briefcase with a jar of honey inside (this was Pooh's idea, as he thought it might help him to think). And they continued playing until they had tried all the different ways of creating new ideas and even a few that they made up themselves, which The Stranger said was perfectly all right and very much in keeping with the rules of which there weren't any (except the part about not being negative). The game really worked. In a very short period of time, they had so many ideas for how to get the briefcase that they had trouble keeping track, and The Stranger had to write them in the dirt so they wouldn't forget them.

"That was fun," said Piglet.

"But quite tiring," said Pooh, "and hungry-making."

"Then we should continue our Problem Solving to retrieve the briefcase," said The Stranger. "The next thing we shall do is to review the different ideas that we have had and choose one that seems the best, think about it more closely and see if we can improve on it, and then try it!" So they talked and talked about the different ideas. Pooh thought the crane idea was a good idea, although he had no idea where they might get a crane. Piglet wanted to fill the Pit with water and float the briefcase out, while The Stranger thought that the String Theory was interesting. In the end they used them all.

Piglet ran and found some string and brought it back to the Pit, where The Stranger was searching for a long stick of just the right type and another short stick that looked like a V.

Pooh walked around and around the Pit, staring down into the darkness and listening to anything the problem might want to say to him and where it might be, until he spotted the briefcase.

"Aha!" said Pooh. "There it is! Right where I thought it would be."

When put together, Pooh's crane idea, Piglet's filling the Pit with water idea, and the String Theory had reminded them all of fishing. Although there was some confuzzlement about whether and what kind of bait a briefcase might like, they set about creating their tool. Pooh broke twigs off the long stick The Stranger had found, Piglet tied one leg of the V-shaped stick to the string, while The Stranger tied the other end of the string to the tip of the long stick.

But try as they might, they didn't have any luck snagging the briefcase. The wooden twig hook would slide across the briefcase, but wouldn't catch it.

"Why isn't it working?" asked Piglet.

"Yes," agreed Pooh. "We've done everything just right and should be on our way to lunch, and yet, here we are, still up at the top of the Pit and the briefcase is still down at the bottom of the Pit and . . ."

"And what we can learn from this," said The Stranger, "is that even if you perform all of the different steps in the Problem-Solving Method exactly, sometimes it just doesn't work when you finally try your solution. Of course, that is a whole subject in itself, and one we shall talk about the next time we are together: the last step in Problem Solving—Employ the Solution and Monitor Results. We shall see that sometimes solutions need to be changed a little once they are put into use if they are to work well."

"But what do we do now?" said Piglet.

"Perhaps if we tied the string to Piglet," said Pooh, "and lowered him down into the Pit, he could attach the hook and then we could both pull the briefcase and Piglet back out again."

"Good idea, Pooh!" said The Stranger.

"Bu-bu-but what if the s-s-string should break?" said Piglet.

"And that's good too, Piglet," said The Stranger. "It's important to think of all the possible consequences of an idea. And it reminds me of when Eeyore joined in your game of Poohsticks. Do you remember?"

Now one day Pooh and Piglet and Rabbit and Roo were all playing Poohsticks together. They had dropped their sticks in when Rabbit said "Go!" and then they had hurried across to the other side of the bridge, and now they were all leaning over the edge, waiting to see whose stick would come out first. But it was a long time coming, because the river was very lazy that day, and hardly seemed to mind if it didn't ever get there at all. . . .

"I can see yours, Piglet," said Pooh suddenly.

"Mine's a sort of greyish one," said Piglet, not daring to lean too far over in case he fell in.

"Yes, that's what I can see. It's coming over on to my side." . . .

"It's coming!" said Pooh.

"Are you *sure* it's mine?" squeaked Piglet excitedly.

"Yes, because it's grey. A big grey one. Here it comes! A very—big—grey—Oh, no, it isn't, it's Eeyore."

And out floated Eeyore.

"Eeyore!" cried everybody.

Looking very calm, very dignified, with his legs in the air, came Eeyore from beneath the bridge. . . .

"I didn't know you were playing," said Roo.

"I'm not," said Eeyore.

"Eeyore, what *are* you doing there?" said Rabbit.

"I'll give you three guesses, Rabbit. Digging holes in the ground? Wrong. Leaping from branch to branch of a young oak-tree? Wrong. Waiting for somebody to help me out of the river? Right. Give Rabbit time, and he'll always get the answer."

"But, Eeyore," said Pooh in distress, "what can we —I mean, how shall we—do you think if we—"

"Yes," said Eeyore. "One of those would be just the thing. Thank you, Pooh."

. . . There was a moment's silence while everybody thought. "I've got a sort of idea," said Pooh at last, "but I don't suppose it's a very good one."

"I don't suppose it is either," said Eeyore.

"Go on, Pooh," said Rabbit. "Let's have it."

"Well, if we all threw stones and things into the river on *one* side of Eeyore, the stones would make waves, and the waves would wash him to the other side."

"That's a very good idea," said Rabbit, and Pooh looked happy again.

"Very," said Eeyore. "When I want to be washed, Pooh, I'll let you know."

"Supposing we hit him by mistake?" said Piglet anxiously.

"Or supposing you missed him by mistake," said Eeyore. "Think of all the possibilities, Piglet, before you settle down to enjoy yourselves."

"And that is the point, Piglet," said The Stranger. "We should think of all the possibilities before we try something."

So they tried tying Piglet to the string and tried lifting him up only a short distance in the air and setting him down again to see if the string would hold, and it did. Then they had Piglet pick up a large stone that The Stranger said would be about the weight of the briefcase, and the string still held, although Piglet was still feeling uneasy about being let down into the Pit. He wasn't quite sure that Pooh had checked completely to see if any Heffalumps might have been trapped there recently.

But Piglet remained brave and Pooh and The Stranger lowered him gently down to the bottom of the Pit, and Piglet attached the hook to the briefcase, stepped on top, and was lifted right out and set gently on the ground.

"Hooray!" they cried.

"We SOLVE'd it! We SOLVE'd it!" cried Piglet, untying himself and running around in circles.

They congratulated one another and walked on to a small clearing next to the river where they sat on some rocks, and The Stranger checked inside the briefcase to make sure nothing had fallen out when it fell into the Pit.

Pooh watched over The Stranger's shoulder, hoping

that there was a forgotten treat inside, but there wasn't.

"So what we have learned today," started The Stranger, "is how to Visualize Possible Solutions, the fourth step in the Problem-Solving Method. We saw how creativity and experience are helpful when trying to think of possible solutions for your problems, and how we use different approaches depending on the type of problem we are trying to solve."

"The Game! We played the Game!" said Piglet.

"That's right," said The Stranger. "We played a Game to help us think of more ideas for ways to solve our problem." Taking out his laptop computer, he showed Pooh and Piglet the different ways that can be used to pretend to change things about a problem:

"We talked about reviewing and selecting problems," continued The Stranger, "and we discussed refining the solution that we chose to make our chance of success even better. And even though we didn't talk about the last step in the Problem-Solving Method—Employ the Solution and Monitor Results—we did get a chance to try out everything that we talked about in rescuing my briefcase from the Very Deep Pit. Thank you both for all your help."

Pooh and Piglet both felt very proud.

The Stranger said good-bye and that he would meet them again on Tuesday, by the Six Tall Trees, if they would like to have lunch with him and learn about Employing and Monitoring Solutions, and then he left.

Pooh and Piglet, after playing a few games of Pooh-sticks, of which Pooh won twenty-three to Piglet's nine-teen, walked to Piglet's house. After the briefest of snacks, as he only wanted just a smackerel to hold him over until he got home, and as the Poohsticks games had been so close and all the excitement had hungered him, Pooh left Piglet's house and began to walk home. And as he walked, he began to hum his Problem-Solving Tune, and even added two new verses. It went something like this:

Select the problem of the day,
Finding one that's right to do,
You can choose it either way,
You pick it or it picks you.

Observe it very carefully,
"Where do I start? Where am I going?"
And don't forget about the bee,
"What's in the way of doing or knowing?"

Learn all you can by asking a lot,
But in the right order, as they are now,
Mostly Whys and then some Whats,
Then Where and When and Who and How.

(And after each, ask Why again.)

Vis-u-a-lize ideas, of course,
We think our thoughts and hope that they
Will put the cart behind the horse,
And not around the other way.

VIII

IN WHICH Employ (the Last and Most
Important Step in the SOLVE
Method) Is Tied Down and Some
Other Things Float Away

"Oh, no!" cried Piglet.

"Oh, no!" cried Pooh.

They watched as The Stranger's picnic basket drifted lazily away from the riverbank.

"Pooh, you pushed the basket into the river!" squeaked Piglet.

"I did not! It fell," said Pooh. "I was just checking it, and it fell."

"Quick, Pooh," said The Stranger, "what is the problem?"

"The problem is that I see lunch moving downstream and sinking lower and lower!"

"Now, Pooh," said The Stranger, "this is your chance to do some really creative Problem Solving, not to mention rescuing our lunch from the river, and us from a hungry walk back. Quick! What do we do first?"

Pooh stared longingly at the hamper as it turned slightly and began to float a little more quickly with the current. "Bother! This problem has selected us! I went to peek inside, not to take anything, mind you, but just to see that there was enough for later . . . and that it was well wrapped up. It must have been perched Very Precariously, or it wouldn't have gone off and fallen into the river."

Pooh continued to follow the progress of the basket, and Piglet did too, as he was walking along the riverbank to keep up with it. "Observing . . . the problem is that my hunger is here in my tummy while my lunch is floating out there. And my goal is to have the lunch and my tummy in the same place, at least for as long as it may take to eat it. And the constraints in this case are *not* bees, but the river, which is wet and wide and not very friendly to bears who cannot swim!"

"Well done, Pooh!" said The Stranger. "That's very good work so far. What shall we do next?"

Pooh wondered for a moment why The Stranger didn't seem upset by the fact that *his* lunch was slowly drifting downstream, but as he was a Bear of Very Little Brain, and since it took all of his concentration to keep up with Piglet without crashing into gorse bushes, he didn't wonder for long.

"Uh . . . next we must ask questions," said Pooh.

"There it is! There it goes!" squealed Piglet, having crawled up onto a rock next to the river to get a better view.

"Why. Why solve this problem?" said Pooh to himself. "Why that's clear, because it's lunchtime. Then we ask What? What is the problem? Well, it is clear that we must rescue the lunch basket from the river before it drifts away and before it sinks. Let's see . . . then we ask Where? Piglet? Where is it going, Piglet?"

"Down, Pooh."

"Yes, but down *where?*" asked Pooh.

"Down the river. I expect it's going to the same place that the river goes, although you can never tell," said Piglet.

"And where does the river go from here?" asked The Stranger.

"It goes out past Kanga's house and the Sand Pit, under the bridge where we play Poohsticks, and on through the Forest," said Piglet.

Pooh wished that the basket *was* a Poohstick, so that they could wait for it at the bridge and then capture it as it went past. "Piglet, when will the basket arrive at the bridge and who will be waiting for it when it does?"

Piglet stopped chasing the progress of the basket long enough to realize that Pooh had a Plan. "Soon, and we will, won't we, Pooh?"

"Yes we will," said Pooh. "Now all we have to figure is the How. Oh, I'm always coming up against Hows."

"What is it, Pooh?" asked The Stranger.

"Well," said Pooh, "I have decided that the basket is following the river and will probably continue to, although you can never be sure, and that it will pass underneath the bridge very soon, where we shall be waiting to rescue it."

"Well done, Pooh," said The Stranger. "And how will you do that?"

"I haven't quite worked it out yet. Perhaps by hooshing, as we did with Eeyore, when he was a Poohstick. Or perhaps the way we rescued your briefcase from the Heffalump trap, by fishing for it, although we haven't any string and I don't think it will wait for us while I send Piglet home to get some. As you see, I'm not quite sure."

"But you are having a great many good ideas," said The Stranger.

"A stick! That's it! A Poohstick!" shouted Piglet.

"What about a Poohstick?" asked Pooh.

"We can use a Poohstick," said Piglet. "A little Bigger and Heavier, but a Poohstick just the same. Will you help us?" Piglet asked, looking at The Stranger.

"Of course," said The Stranger. "What is it you want me to do?"

"I thought," said Piglet, trying to explain and keep an eye on the basket as they walked along, "that we could use Pooh's Plan, and go to the bridge, and you could use a stick to fish the basket out of the river while Pooh and I held onto your legs to keep you from falling in."

"Splendid, Piglet!" said Pooh.

"So now we have a Plan," said The Stranger. "And it sounds like a Very Clever Plan, indeed. And this reminds me of the time of the flood. Do you remember?"

"How could I forget!" said Piglet, and he shivered.

"Yes," said The Stranger, "and your adventures then and our problem now are just the thing I was going to talk to you about today before my basket fell into the river."

"It was pushed!" said Piglet.

"It fell!" said Pooh.

"No matter," continued The Stranger. "What I was going to tell you about was the last and most important step in the Problem-Solving Method: Employ the Solution and Monitor Results."

"Why is it the most important step?" asked Piglet.

"Because," said The Stranger, "of all that has gone before. We have done a great deal of work to get to the last step, and all of our efforts will be wasted if we don't Employ our Solution."

"So what do we have to do?" asked Pooh.

"Once you have Selected," continued The Stranger, "Observed and Learned all about your problem, and you have Visualized Possible Solutions and chosen one, the final step is to put that solution into place. The way that is done is to 'create a path from here to there,' then 'test on a small scale,' and finally to 'Employ Your Solution and Monitor Results.' "

"Creating paths and testing scales," said Pooh. "That sounds like it could take a long time. I fear the basket won't slow down long enough to let you finish doing all that before it goes past the bridge."

"No, no, no," said The Stranger. "This won't take long,

and we can talk as we go. When we are ready to Employ the Solution we've come up with, the first thing we do is to 'create a path from here to there.' That is another way of saying that we develop an action plan. An Action Plan is a summary of all the things that we need to do or to assemble to be ready to implement our plan. Remember when Piglet was stuck inside his house by the flood?"

So as they walked alongside the river, with Piglet scrambling up and down among the rocks and bushes next to the edge, the better to keep sight of the basket, lazily drifting with the current, The Stranger told the story again of how it had rained for days and days, how the water had risen in the Forest, and how Piglet had found himself surrounded by water and trapped in his home.

"It's a little Anxious," he said to himself, "to be a Very Small Animal Entirely Surrounded by Water. Christopher Robin and Pooh could escape by Climbing Trees, and Kanga could escape by Jumping, and Rabbit could escape by Burrowing, and Owl could escape by Flying, and Eeyore could escape by—by Making a Loud Noise Until Rescued, and here am I, surrounded by water and I can't do *anything*."

It went on raining, and every day the water got a little higher, until now it was nearly up to Piglet's window . . . and still he hadn't done anything.

"There's Pooh," he thought to himself. "Pooh hasn't much brain, but he never comes to any harm. He does silly things and they turn out right. There's Owl. Owl

hasn't exactly got Brain, but he Knows Things. He
would know the Right Thing to Do when Surrounded
by Water. There's Rabbit. He hasn't Learnt in Books,
but he can always Think of a Clever Plan. There's
Kanga. She isn't Clever, Kanga isn't, but she would be
so anxious about Roo that she would do a Good Thing

to Do without thinking about it. And then there's Eeyore. And Eeyore is so miserable anyhow that he wouldn't mind about this. But I wonder what Christopher Robin would do?"

Then suddenly he remembered a story which Christopher Robin had told him about a man on a desert island who had written something in a bottle and thrown it in the sea; and Piglet thought that if he wrote something in a bottle and threw it in the water, perhaps somebody would come and rescue *him!*

He left the window and began to search his house, all of it that wasn't under water, and at last he found a pencil and a small piece of dry paper, and a bottle with a cork to it. And he wrote on one side of the paper:

HELP!

PIGLET (ME)

and on the other side:

IT'S ME PIGLET, HELP HELP.

Then he put the paper in the bottle, and he corked the bottle up as tightly as he could, and he leant out of

his window as far as he could lean without falling in, and he threw the bottle as far as he could throw— *splash!*—and in a little while it bobbed up again on the water; and he watched it floating slowly away in the distance, until his eyes ached with looking, and sometimes he thought it was the bottle, and sometimes he thought it was just a ripple on the water which he was following, and then suddenly he knew that he would never see it again and that he had done all that he could do to save himself.

When The Stranger had finished, he and Pooh walked along in silence for a moment or two. They could see the bridge up ahead around a bend in the river and with the sight of it Pooh's heart leaped, or perhaps it was his tummy, at the prospect of being close to the successful conclusion of this adventure. So he hoped.

"So you can see that Piglet does an excellent job of using someone else's solution, in this case a story that Christopher Robin had told him, to solve his own problem." At this Piglet stopped his scrambling along the riverside for a moment and smiled proudly. "But more important for us, we see that once he had settled on his plan, using a note in a bottle to call for help, he necessarily had to have a note, for which he would need a pencil, and a piece of paper, and a bottle in which to place it."

"And a cork!" added Piglet.

"That's right," said The Stranger, "and a cork to keep

the note dry and to allow the bottle to float. Having assembled his paper, pencil, bottle—"

"And cork!" said Piglet.

"—and cork," continued The Stranger, "he had to sit down and write the note, place the note inside the bottle, cork it tightly, and then throw it as far as he could out of his window. Each one of those things was an Action taken by Piglet to put his plan to work. Hence the term Action Plan, which is another way of saying 'creating a path from here to there.' "

Pooh thought about what The Stranger had said, but mostly he thought about the word "Hence," for he liked the sound of it, and it seemed to be the kind of word that Owl might use.

"So when we have chosen a solution," continued The Stranger, "we create an Action Plan that lists all of the things we must get or do to be able to put our plan into use. Now you have said that to rescue our basket, you want me to use a stick and lean over the bridge while you hold me, and I am to snag the basket. What is our Action Plan?"

"We must get to the bridge first!" said Piglet, hurrying now.

"And we must find a stick," said Pooh. "And it must be a Special Poohstick. One that is Bigger and Longer than most."

The Stranger hurried to keep up, and Pooh and Piglet raced ahead, with Piglet running up onto the bridge and turning to look back upstream for the basket. Pooh had turned off before reaching the bridge and was searching around on the ground for just the right stick as The Stranger arrived.

"I see it! I see it!" cried Piglet.

The Stranger leaned forward over the railing to look as Pooh came up with a stick that would be no good at all for Poohsticks, but which he thought would be right for fishing baskets out of rivers.

The basket was still upstream. "Here, Pooh," The Stranger said, "give me the stick and I shall tell you about the next part of Employing the Solution, while I practice. That is called 'testing on a small scale.'" And with this, The Stranger took the stick and got down on the bridge, leaning through the railings while holding the stick in one hand.

"But what are you doing? The basket isn't here yet," said Piglet.

"Now that we have done everything our Action Plan called for," said The Stranger, "it is often useful, especially with large or complex problems, to try them out in a very small way to see if they work before committing yourself to them completely. That way, if the solution doesn't work exactly as you had thought, you have the chance to alter or modify it before using it in a big way. Like this."

The Stranger asked Pooh and Piglet to hold tight to his legs as he stretched out and began to swing the stick back and forth. He was able to touch the end of the stick into the river, and splashed back and forth once or twice to get the feel of it. And then he tried to pretend that he was snagging a basket just to see how it might go. After a minute, he got up.

"There," he said, "that was quite good. I was testing our solution to see how it might work, and I think it might work just fine."

Pooh was very happy, as it meant that he might soon have something to eat, which he needed quite badly now, what with all the excitement and Problem Solving that he had been doing. The Stranger continued to explain.

"When we begin to Employ a Solution, we want to test on a small scale. The reason we do this is that it allows us to conserve resources and make sure our solution is a good one before we fully commit to it. We will use the same method when we are testing on a small scale as when we are employing a full-scale solution. We need to remember what our goal was so that we can be sure just exactly how we define success, and we need to select criteria that we will use to measure the results of our solution."

"What's a criteria?" asked Piglet.

"That's a place where you stand in line and pick out all your favorite foods," said Pooh, remembering what Christopher Robin had told him about it.

"No, Pooh," said The Stranger, "that's something else altogether. Criteria are standards we can use to judge whether or not our solution was successful. Like a yardstick."

Pooh knew all about yardsticks, but only so far as they made excellent pirate swords and were also useful for pushing your paper boats away from the sides of streams where they had gotten stuck on twigs and roots and such.

"For this problem," continued The Stranger, "we could use as criteria whether or not we snag the basket, whether or not the contents have gotten wet, or if they have, how much of them. Those are all things we can check after we Employ our Solution to see just how successful we have been."

"What if we aren't able to snag the basket?" asked Piglet.

"We shall all starve," said Pooh seriously.

"That's a good point, Piglet," said The Stranger. "When we are beginning to Employ our Solution, it is a good idea to have a fallback option in mind. If things do not go very well, we have an alternative that we've thought of beforehand. To be prepared."

"So if we miss the basket," said Piglet, "a fallback option would be that we go farther downstream and begin hooshing the basket."

"Yes," said The Stranger. "But let's hope our solution doesn't require that. How soon till it arrives, Piglet?"

"It's moving rather slowly," said Piglet, "but I would think another minute or two before it arrives."

"Well then," said The Stranger, "I just have time to remember a little more of the story about the flood and your rescue of Piglet."

And so The Stranger continued the story:

And it was on the morning of the fourth day that Piglet's bottle came floating past him, and with one loud cry of "Honey!" Pooh plunged into the water, seized the bottle, and struggled back to his tree again.

"Bother!" said Pooh, as he opened it. "All that wet for nothing. What's that bit of paper doing?"

He took it out and looked at it.

"It's a Missage," he said to himself, "that's what it is. And that letter is a 'P,' and so is that, and so is that, and 'P' means 'Pooh,' so it's a very important Missage to me, and I can't read it. I must find Christopher Robin or Owl or Piglet, one of those Clever Readers who can read things, and they will tell me what this missage means. Only I can't swim. Bother!"

Then he had an idea, and I think that for a Bear of Very Little Brain, it was a good idea. He said to himself:

"If a bottle can float, then a jar can float, and if a

jar floats, I can sit on the top of it, if it's a very big jar."

So he took his biggest jar, and corked it up. "All boats have to have a name," he said, "so I shall call mine The Floating Bear." And with these words he dropped his boat into the water and jumped in after it.

For a little while Pooh and *The Floating Bear* were uncertain as to which of them was meant to be on the top, but after trying one or two different positions, they settled down with *The Floating Bear* underneath and Pooh triumphantly astride it, paddling vigorously with his feet.

"If I had *The Floating Bear* here," said Pooh, "I would be able to go and rescue the basket straight away!"

"But the part of this story that I wanted to share," said the Stranger, "was the part where, after you had chosen your solution, *The Floating Bear,* you still had to change your position several times before you got the hang of it. And that changing, once you've Employed a Solution, is very useful to Problem Solving. One mustn't be so attached to a particular solution that it isn't changed for the better as you go along."

"Here it comes!" squeaked Piglet. "Get ready!"

"One more thing," said The Stranger. "When we Employ the Solution we've chosen, it is important to really watch for signs as to whether the solution is working or not. When we see or hear that our solution is not working, or not working as well as we would like, we can still change and adapt it, whereas if we aren't open to the signs, our solution could fail and we wouldn't have a clue as to why. This is called 'feedback,' and—"

"Feedback!" said Pooh. "That's a part of Communication too! I remember that from learning how to be a V.I.B. (Very Important Bear) and a manager."

"That's right," said The Stranger. "And it serves the same purpose here, to allow you to monitor the progress of your solution as it is implemented, or Employed."

"Here it is! Here it is!" cried Piglet, jumping up and down frantically although the basket was still approaching the bridge, drifting lazily in the current.

"It doesn't seem right, somehow," said Pooh. "I think it is going to pass under the bridge toward that end."

"Very good, Pooh," said The Stranger. "Then let us adjust our solution, based on your feedback, and move over there."

The Stranger went to where the basket was likely to pass and got down and prepared to lean out with the stick in his hand to reach for the basket. Piglet and Pooh grabbed on to his legs to hold him steady, but The Stranger was much bigger than your average animal in the Forest, not to mention your average Piglet in the Forest, so it was not an easy thing. As the basket came closer, it started to swirl and spin from the currents next to the bridge.

"Wait," said The Stranger, "move a little left!"

Since he was upside down and even on the best of days was still confused about which was left and which was right, Pooh asked tentatively, "To the left?"

"Right."

"Right?" cried Pooh.

"No. To the left!"

"Help!" cried Piglet, who was holding fast to The Stranger's cuff but was being tossed to and fro for his trouble.

"A little farther out now!" cried The Stranger. "I've almost got it!"

"Is out left or right?" Pooh asked Piglet.

"Wait, no . . . just a little more . . . hold on, I'm starting to slip. . . ."

"It must be left, that sounds right," said Pooh.

"I'm slipping!" shouted The Stranger.

"I think he's feeding back," observed Piglet.

"Should we adjust something?" asked Pooh.

"Help! Help!" cried Piglet, who was losing his grip on The Stranger's cuff.

SPLASH!

"Is that what they call a Fallback?" asked Piglet as he

and Pooh stood by the railing and stared down at the river.

And with the splash, Rabbit and Roo came bounding out of the woods and ran up to where Pooh and Piglet were leaning over the railing, staring at where The Stranger had been only a moment before. "Can we help? We heard the shouting and came as quickly as we could."

The Stranger bobbed to the surface with the stick in one hand and the basket in his other.

"Should we start Hooshing?" shouted Pooh.

The Stranger didn't answer but waded to the bank.

Pooh and Piglet and Rabbit and Roo all hurried off the bridge and down to where The Stranger had come ashore, set the basket on a stump, and was shaking the water off his clothes.

They were all silent. No one was quite sure what The Stranger might do.

"I . . . uh . . . I'm sorry," stammered Pooh. "I thought we had a better grip. And then there was the shouting, and you said 'right,' and I thought you meant left, I mean, you said. . . ."

"That's all right, Pooh," said The Stranger. "One thing about solving problems, sometimes you get wet. But did you learn anything?"

"I learned something!" Piglet said, jumping up now that he saw that The Stranger wasn't going to get angry. "I learned that next time we do this, you should try to grab the basket without falling in."

"Thank you, Piglet."

"So, I guess we failed at solving the problem," said Pooh sadly.

"Well," said The Stranger, "what do you think? What was our goal?"

"To rescue the basket?" said Pooh.

"And did we?" asked The Stranger.

"Uh, yes . . ." said Pooh slowly.

"And how else did we say that we would judge our success?" asked The Stranger.

"Our cafeteria!" shouted Piglet, at which point Rabbit

and Roo cast glances at each other, not quite understanding what was going on.

"Criteria."

"We said," said Pooh, brightening, "that getting the basket out was one part . . . and that whether or not the food was wet was another," he said, the words coming faster as he realized, "and if it was wet, how much . . ." Pooh opened the top of the basket and began pawing through the contents.

"Success! We solved it!" he cried, and lifted a wet but intact jar of honey out of the basket. "The sandwiches and things were packed on top of this jar, and just like *The Floating Bear*, it must have floated and kept the basket up."

"So," said The Stranger, "based on what we said was the goal and the criteria against which we would measure our solution, this *was* a success."

"But you got all wet!" said Piglet.

"Yes, that's true," said The Stranger. "And next time, I'm going to make sure that one of the constraints is Not Getting Wet." The Stranger laughed and began to unload the picnic hamper while Piglet told Rabbit and Roo all about the adventure and how Pooh and he had solved the problem all by themselves.

Meanwhile, Pooh was not heard to say much of anything more than "Mmmmmmm, Hmmmmm," and "Hmmmmmm, Mmmmmmm."

"But let's finish the story about the flood," said The Stranger when Piglet had come to the end of his explanation. "And you'll see that Pooh has some experience at testing things on a small scale, as he has done it before." And The Stranger told the rest of the tale.

"Now then, Pooh," said Christopher Robin, "where's your boat?"

"I ought to say," explained Pooh as they walked down to the shore of the island, "that it isn't just an ordinary sort of boat. Sometimes it's a Boat, and sometimes it's more of an Accident. It all depends."

"Depends on what?"

"On whether I'm on the top of it or underneath it."

"Oh! Well, where is it?"

"There!" said Pooh, pointing proudly to *The Floating Bear*.

It wasn't what Christopher Robin expected, and the more he looked at it, the more he thought what a Brave and Clever Bear Pooh was, and the more Christopher Robin thought this, the more Pooh looked modestly down his nose and tried to pretend he wasn't.

"But it's too small for two of us," said Christopher Robin sadly.

"Three of us with Piglet."

"That makes it smaller still. Oh, Pooh Bear, what shall we do?"

And then this Bear, Pooh Bear, Winnie-the-Pooh, F.O.P. (Friend of Piglet's), R.C. (Rabbit's Companion), P.D. (Pole Discoverer), E.C. and T.F. (Eeyore's Comforter and Tail-Finder)—in fact, Pooh himself—said something so clever that Christopher Robin could only look at him with mouth open and eyes staring, wondering if this was really the Bear of Very Little Brain whom he had known and loved so long.

"We might go in your umbrella," said Pooh.

"?"

"We might go in your umbrella," said Pooh.

"??"

"We might go in your umbrella," said Pooh.

"!!!!!!"

For suddenly Christopher Robin saw that they might. He opened his umbrella and put it point downwards in the water. It floated but wobbled. Pooh got in. He was just beginning to say that it was all right now, when he found that it wasn't, so after a short drink which he didn't really want he waded back to Christopher Robin. Then they both got in together, and it wobbled no longer.

"I shall call this boat *The Brain of Pooh*," said Christopher Robin, and *The Brain of Pooh* set sail forthwith in a south-westerly direction, revolving gracefully.

You can imagine [Piglet's] joy when at last he saw the good ship, *The Brain of Pooh* (*Captain*, C. Robin; *1st Mate*, P. Bear) coming over the sea to rescue him.

"So *The Brain of Pooh* was your solution to how to rescue Piglet," said The Stranger. "And having chosen that solution, you went about testing it by getting inside and trying it out before you and Christopher Robin committed yourselves to setting off in search of Piglet."

"And a good thing too," said Pooh. "I found that the umbrella was quite tippy, unless of course you had *both* a captain and a first mate on board."

"And that's just the type of thing that testing on a small scale can do for you when you are using it to try and solve a problem."

So they ate their lunch, and Pooh, having finished his honey, and before starting on some bread with condensed milk, sang his Problem-Solving Rhyme, and even added a last verse:

> *Employ the best idea found,*
> *And watch what happens most precisely,*
> *Making sure by looking round,*
> *That things are working out quite nicely.*

After they had finished, The Stranger got up and thanked Pooh and Piglet for their help but said he had to leave as he was still quite wet and needed to go home and change before he got the wheezles and sneezles.

"But before I go," said The Stranger, "I'd like to review what we talked about regarding the final step in the Problem-Solving Method: Employ the Solution and Monitor Results. That having Visualized and Selected a Solution in the previous step, we begin by Creating an Action Plan."

"Which is another way of saying 'creating a path from here to there,' " said Piglet to Roo in exactly the tone of voice he had heard used when he rode in Christopher Robin's pocket and went to school.

"That's right," said The Stranger. "And the next part is Testing on a Small Scale, where we try out the solution in a small way to see how well it works. We do this by defining exactly what success is and developing criteria . . ."

"That's like a yardstick," Pooh whispered to Rabbit, "for measuring."

". . . that we use to judge our relative success. We make changes in our solution as they are warranted while we are Employing it, and we try to have a fallback option in case things go wrong."

"Although falling back in the water is Not Desired," said Pooh.

"So true, Pooh," said The Stranger. "Once we have tested successfully on a small scale, we use the same process to Employ our Solution full scale, and we continue to Monitor the Results, being alert for any feedback that would indicate a change might be necessary. If you have followed all of the steps to this point, your solution will be Employed easily, and your problem will be solved."

"Hence, you have lunch," said Pooh proudly.

IX

IN WHICH The Stranger Takes Everyone on an Adventure, Piglet Finds a Fair-sized Problem, and Pooh SOLVEs It

"The Fair! The Fair!" squeaked Piglet, scurrying ahead of the others toward the entrance booth, with Roo trailing slightly behind crying "Oh! Oh!" and acting Very Excited.

"It will rain," said Eeyore, looking up at the cloudless sky. "Sun in the morning; rain without warning. That's what they say."

"Thank you very much for bringing us," said Pooh to The Stranger.

"Not at all, Pooh," said The Stranger. "It is the least I could do, since all of you have helped me so much with my work. And going to a Country Fair is one of my favorite things to do."

"Tiggers like fairs best," said Tigger.

"And I shall enjoy the exhibitions," said Owl. "Did I ever tell you about the time that my great uncle Horace won the blue ribbon at a fair for Best of Show? It was during the fall of the Rainy Year . . ."

While The Stranger went to buy tickets, the others listened to Owl, and Pooh stared with wonder at the fair. The Stranger had heard about the pageant and fair that was being held in a clearing near the village, on the other side of the Forest from the Hundred Acre Wood. He had invited everyone to join him for an afternoon. They waited for The Stranger to return with the tickets and stared at the brightly colored tents, banners, and flags. At the center of the small grouping of tents was a gently turning Ferris wheel. It was almost as tall as the Bee Tree. They watched as the wheel swung lazily around, and listened to the music from the wheel drifting across the fairgrounds.

Tigger went off in search of whatever it is Tiggers like best at fairs, and Owl and Eeyore went to one of the tents. Pooh, Piglet, Rabbit, Roo, and The Stranger walked along, taking in the sights and sounds of the fair.

"I think I shall get some popcorn," said The Stranger. "Would you like anything, Pooh? Piglet? Rabbit? Roo?"

"No, thank you," said Rabbit. "I am going to ride the Ferris wheel, and I shall want to have my hands free."

"Me too!" said Roo.

"All right," said The Stranger. "We'll meet at the Ferris wheel."

And The Stranger walked off toward the concession stand.

"Would you like to come with us, Pooh?" asked Rabbit.

"No, thank you," said Pooh. "I have been thinking of a hum about the fair, and I think I shall stay here and hum it until it is fully Thought."

"What about you, Piglet?"

Piglet looked at the wheel. It looked very high.

"No," he said. "I think I'll stay with Pooh in case he needs help with his hum."

Roo and Rabbit hurried off toward the Ferris wheel.

"Wave to us when you get up to the very top!" Pooh called after them.

"We shall," Roo squeaked.

Pooh and Piglet sat down on a bench and watched the people walk by while Pooh thought of his hum and waited for The Stranger to return. Piglet noticed that Rabbit and Roo were on the Ferris wheel at the very top, and he could just make out the two tiny figures sitting in the seat, waving and waving. Piglet waved back.

Pooh waited for more of his hum to come to him. When he looked up, he too noticed that Rabbit and Roo were at the very top of the wheel and were waving at him. He waved back.

Pooh thought he saw The Stranger returning from the concession stand, but it turned out to be someone else. Piglet looked up again, and Rabbit and Roo were *still* at the very top of the wheel and were waving just as hard as before. They must be having a grand time he thought, and he continued to watch, wanting to see the wheel as it turned round.

But the wheel did not turn.

Rabbit and Roo continued to wave and wave. Piglet thought this was Very Strange. Usually Ferris wheels went around and around all the time. Or at least that was his impression from what Christopher Robin had told him. But as he watched, the Ferris wheel did not move, and Rabbit and Roo continued to be in the seat at the very top of the wheel and continued to wave and wave their arms. Piglet decided to go see.

"Pooh? I think I may have found a problem," said Piglet.

"And what is that, Piglet?" said Pooh.

"Come with me to the Ferris wheel and we shall see," said Piglet.

As Piglet and Pooh made their way toward the Ferris wheel, Tigger came bouncing up to them. "Pooh! Piglet! Come quick! The Ferris wheel is stuck and Rabbit and Roo are on it, so they have become stuck as well!" So with Tigger leading the way through the crowd, Pooh and Piglet hurried to the wheel.

When they arrived, the wheel operator was standing next to the control lever that started and stopped the wheel, looking up, and wiping his brow with a handkerchief.

"What has happened?" asked Pooh.

"I don't know," said the operator. "Everything was working fine, and then all of a sudden the gears jammed, and it stopped."

Pooh looked up and could see Rabbit and Roo in the seat at the very top of the wheel, rocking back and forth as they waved and waved their arms. He couldn't quite hear what they were calling, if they were calling at all. Perhaps they weren't worried yet, thinking that this must just be part of Riding a Ferris wheel.

"Don't worry," Piglet called up to the pair, just in case they knew they were stuck. "We'll get you down," he added, though he wasn't quite sure how just yet. But it was always helpful to be comforting.

Just then, Owl and Eeyore rushed up following Tigger, who had gone to fetch them.

"What . . . what has happened?" asked Owl, gasping from the hurry.

"Rabbit and Roo have become stuck at the top of the Ferris wheel!" said Pooh. "This is a problem."

"I knew it," said Eeyore gloomily. "I knew it was too good to be true. I should have known it was the kind of day for a problem."

"Is there anything you can do?" asked Pooh of the operator.

"Not until they send someone to repair it. It could take hours," said the operator. "Lucky that only your friends were on at the time. I was just about to load some more people when it stopped."

Pooh didn't know why the operator thought it was lucky that Rabbit and Roo were stuck, as it didn't seem to be the kind of thing that Pooh thought was lucky at all.

"They do seem," said Owl, "to be ensconced in an unreachable aerie, at the zenith of this cyclical transport."

"And they're stuck at the top of the ride too," said Tigger.

"So we must rescue them," said Pooh firmly. "This is a problem, and we shall SOLVE it!"

"What do we do first?" asked Tigger, who, because of his bounciness during the many discussions on Problem Solving with The Stranger, hadn't paid proper attention, and so was quite unsure where to start.

"The first step," said Pooh confidently, "is to Select the Problem. The S step from SOLVE."

"It seems that the problem—" Eeyore started to say.

"—selected us," finished Piglet excitedly.

Pooh began to hum his problem-solving hum to himself. When he got to the second verse he said slowly, "The next step is to Observe. . . . Observe, Organize, and Define the Problem. Just *What* is the problem?"

"The problem is," said Owl, "that Rabbit and Roo are entrapped at the top!"

"And the wheel can't move," added Tigger.

"And it doesn't look good," said Eeyore.

"It will be hours," said Piglet, squeaking faster and faster, "before they are able to get a repair crew here to fix it, and both Rabbit and Roo are Very Excitable. I don't think that they will be very happy when they realize what has happened. We *must* find a way to get them down."

"Without falling," said Tigger. "That's a constraint, remember?"

"Good," said Pooh, wishing he weren't a Bear of Very Little Brain, and hoping he had learned enough about solving problems. "And what are we starting with?"

"We have everything one might have," said Owl, "if he were at a Country Fair."

"And there are all of us," said Tigger. He looked around and some people were looking up and pointing at the two very small figures in the seat at the very top of the wheel, waving their arms and rocking their seat back and forth.

"So what shall we do next?" asked Eeyore. "Not that it likely will do any good, but I suppose we should try."

"The next step is to Learn by Questioning," said Pooh. "We must ask the five W's and How? in the right order, and try to understand more about the problem. Does anyone remember the correct order?" Pooh stared at the blank faces before him. "Let me think."

Pooh thought for a good long minute. Actually, he hummed. He hummed to himself the next verse of his Problem-Solving Hum, remembering that when he had made it up, he had been very careful about the order of the five W's and How so that he would always remember them. Like now.

> *Learn all you can by asking a lot,*
> *But in the right order, as they are now,*
> *Mostly Whys and then some Whats,*
> *Then Where and When and Who and How.*
>
> *(And after each, ask Why again.)*

"I have it," said Pooh. And he explained the five W's and How? to the others in the correct order so that they could help him. "We know the Why of the problem, as we want to get Rabbit and Roo down safely because they are our friends. So let's start with the What."

"What is keeping the wheel from moving?" asked Eeyore.

They all looked at the operator. "The gears have jammed," he said.

"And Why?" asked Pooh, remembering that this was always a good question to ask, no matter what.

"I think because the drive belt broke and pieces of it fell in between the gears," said the operator.

The animals all looked at one another. None of them, except Owl of course, knew anything at all about gears and drive belts, and at this point Owl was being quiet as he wanted to be quite sure before he said anything.

"Is there a way to make it move without the motor?" asked Tigger.

"Very good, Tigger," said Pooh.

"I don't think so," said the operator. "The automatic brake has engaged and until we fix the motor and the gears, we won't be able to move the wheel."

"Oh," they all said.

Pooh stepped back and looked up at the top of the wheel. Rabbit and Roo were still waving their arms and rocking back and forth.

"Where is The Stranger?" asked Pooh, looking back toward the concession stand where he had last seen him. "I do wish he were here to help. *He* would know what to do."

"Ahem! In previous occurrences of this type, that is *When* this happened before, what did you do?" asked Owl. Pooh was pleased that Owl had asked a When question, and just at the right time.

"Mostly we just waited for the repair crew," said the operator. "When the people were finally able to get off, we tried to make it up to them by offering them free rides, but not many usually took them."

"I'm not surprised," said Eeyore.

"Who can fix the wheel?" asked Pooh. "And how do they do it?"

"I don't know," said the operator.

"Why do they leave the people on while they fix it?" Tigger asked.

"I don't think they do," said the operator. "They usually get them off first so that there's no load on the motor."

"But how do they do that?" asked Piglet. "And can we do that now?"

"I wish we could," said the operator, "but you see, the repair crew has a special tool they use . . ." and on and on he went talking about extension ladders, flywheels, and centrifugal brakes and other things that Pooh was sure he didn't know the least thing about.

Finally, the operator finished his explanation and Owl nodded wisely as though he had understood.

"So," asked Pooh, "can you get them down?"

"No," said the operator.

"Just as I thought," said Eeyore.

"I too," said Owl. "An irreducible conundrum, with a dearth of expeditious alternatives."

"Well, we did find out that the wheel won't move," said Pooh, looking about again for The Stranger and wishing he were there. "Tigger? Would you be so kind as to bounce off and search for The Stranger? I think he could help us a great deal, but it seems that he has misplaced himself."

"Tiggers are good at finding people. Especially at a Fair," said Tigger. He bounded off with a "Worraworra-worraworra."

"Now let me see," said Pooh. "We have arrived at the

point where we know about the problem and must Visualize Possible Solutions, Select One, and Refine It. . . . Do any of you have any thoughts? Oh, I wish Christopher Robin were here. I always seem to have much better thoughts when he is around."

"Why don't you just ask Owl to fly up to the top of the Ferris wheel and bring them down?" asked Eeyore. "The simplest thing. I should have thought of it sooner, but I was thinking about the rain, which will be coming down any minute now."

"Ahem," said Owl, preparing to give his now well-practiced speech on the Necessary Dorsal Muscles, when Pooh interrupted.

"That's a good idea, Eeyore. Do you have any more?" said Pooh. "The more ideas we have, the better our chance of success."

"I shan't be able to rescue Rabbit," said Owl, "but I might be able to help Roo, who is quite a bit smaller and not so much a strain on the Necessary Dors—"

"Another idea!" exclaimed Pooh. "Very good. Things are beginning to look up!" At which point Eeyore and Owl looked up, for this was what they thought Pooh had wanted, and when Tigger bounced up, he too looked up.

"Tigger, did you find The Stranger?" asked Pooh.

"Finding strangers is what Tiggers do best," he said. "But Tiggers do much better finding strangers in the woods, where there aren't so many strangers about."

"We shall just have to come up with more ideas ourselves," said Pooh. "What if we tried something that has helped rescue someone before?"

"Like a note in a bottle?" asked Piglet.

"We could try standing on one another's shoulders. Except for the fact that it might snap my back in two, because naturally I'd be on the bottom," said Eeyore.

"If Christopher Robin were here, we could use his tunic and let Rabbit and Roo jump into it," said Tigger.

"That would never work," said Eeyore. "They're much too high."

"Now, Eeyore," said Pooh gently, "when we are thinking of ideas, it is important that we remember the rule that we not criticize them right away. Because even bad ideas might remind us of good ones and we don't want to lose any good ones, remember?" Tigger felt better because it had been his idea, and Eeyore felt worse because he had been corrected, but then he had expected it.

"I'm out of ideas, Pooh," said Piglet.

"Well, then," said Pooh, "we should try those techniques that The Stranger taught us to get more ideas. Let's see . . . the first one was . . . make it bigger . . . I think."

"If the Ferris wheel were bigger," said Piglet, "I think we should never get them down."

"And if they were bigger," said Eeyore, "the wheel would snap like a donkey's back and they *would* be down."

"I don't think this is working so well," said Piglet.

"We must give it time," said Pooh. "Now the next thing was to make something smaller."

"If the wheel were smaller," said Eeyore, "that would be the same as if they were bigger. No help at all."

"And if they were smaller," said Tigger, "they could crawl down all by themselves."

"Could they really do that?" said Pooh.

"Ants do," said Tigger. "Climb trees, that is."

"But do you think," said Pooh, looking up again at the two small figures, "that they might be able to climb down themselves?"

"I don't think Roos are built for climbing," said Piglet.

"Or Rabbits," said Tigger.

"Or Donkeys," said Eeyore.

"Then we must continue thinking of ideas," said Pooh. "The next technique, I think, was to reverse something."

"If we could reverse the wheel, we could bring them right down," said Piglet. "But the operator said we couldn't."

"I think what The Stranger meant," said Piglet, "is that we reverse one part of the problem, like . . ."

"Like figuring out how to get Rabbit and Roo up there," said Eeyore, "instead of trying to get them down."

"Exactly," said Pooh.

"That gives me an idea!" shouted Piglet. "Remember

during the Great Blusterous Day? When we went to visit Owl and his house decided to reverse itself?"

"Of course," said Owl. "There is nothing wrong with my memory. Tell me about it again. The parts that interest you, of course."

"The house was upside down," Piglet explained, talking faster and faster as he went on, from excitement, "and the door was on the ceiling, and we had to get out, and we didn't know quite how we would do it, and I was small but Owl's Necessary Dorsal Muscles were the same as they are now and the letter-box was small and so we sent Owl up with the string and then pulled me up to get Christopher Robin."

Piglet stood panting, expectantly waiting for a response. "Don't you see, what if we were to put a string up to the top of the wheel? Then we could tie it to me and pull me up and . . . Oh. I guess that wouldn't work after all. It would just get me stuck up there with them."

"Lowering," said Eeyore.

"Yes, that's it!" said Piglet. "What if we used the string for *lowering* Rabbit and Roo, instead of raising them like they did with me?"

"No," said Eeyore. "I meant the skies are lowering. I think it's going to rain after all."

"Still," said Pooh, "that's a Very Good Idea, Piglet."

Piglet felt especially proud, for not only had he had a Very Good Idea, but he wouldn't have to be tied to a string and raised up very high. Which he remembered, but not fondly.

"And that is the Best Idea yet," said Pooh. "Tell us again, Piglet, so that we can Refine and Improve It."

"I just thought . . . I mean, if we could just . . ." Piglet stammered, stopped, and then started all over again after taking a deep breath. "My Very Good Idea is that we should get a string and use it for lowering Rabbit and Roo from the top of the Ferris wheel in just the opposite way that I was raised to the letter box."

"That *is* a Very Good Plan," said Pooh after a moment's reflection. "But I'm still having trouble with the Hows. How do we get the string up there, and How do we lower them, and How . . ."

"We shall need to get a very long piece of string," said Piglet. "And we shall need to have Owl fly it up to the top of the wheel. And we shall need to loop it over, and we shall need him to explain our Plan to Rabbit and Roo."

"That is an improvement," said Owl.

"And we must hurry!" Pooh said.

"Before it rains," said Eeyore.

Pooh looked up and noticed that the two very small figures in the seat at the very top of the Ferris wheel had stopped waving and rocking and were just sitting there.

"The next step is . . ." And here Pooh paused and tried hard to remember just what it was that was the next step, and surprised even himself, a Bear of Very Little Brain, when he said, "Employ the Solution and Monitor Results! The last step of the SOLVE Problem-Solving Method."

"Oh, boy!" said Piglet. "We need an Action Plan!"

"Action Plans are what Tiggers do best," said Tigger. "What's an Action Plan?"

"It's a plan of action," said Owl.

"Oh."

"We shall need some string," said Eeyore. "Waterproof, preferably."

"And we shall have to test it," said Piglet, remembering how they had tested the string when The Stranger's briefcase had fallen into the Very Deep Pit.

"And we shall have to think about what to tell Rabbit and Roo when I fly up there," said Owl.

"This is a Very Good Action Plan," said Pooh. "Let's begin. Tigger, can you go find a very long piece of string?"

"Finding string is what Tiggers do best," and he bounced off toward the midway.

Within moments he was back to the surprise of all with a large bobbin of string that he had found, saying that he had explained the problem to the balloon man, who had offered to help by giving him the whole ball of balloon string.

"Pooh?" said Piglet. "I think I have found a constraint."

"What is that?" said Pooh.

"It is a thing which keeps you from doing something," said Piglet.

"No, no, I know that," said Pooh. "I mean, what is the constraint that you have found?"

"I don't think that string will hold them," said Piglet.

"At least not Rabbit, who is much larger than I, although it may hold Roo, who is much smaller than I."

Pooh thought for a moment. "Then we shall have to try it on a small scale first. To see if it works." So Pooh led the others over to a tent and tied the string to a small scale they found there. It was just about the size of Roo, but because it was made of metal was about as heavy as Piglet, and with all of them pulling together, they tried to lift it. *Snap!* The string broke.

"Like a Donkey's back," said Eeyore.

"You were right, Piglet," said Pooh. "Now we shall have to try something else."

"If we made it bigger," said Owl, "the string, that is, it would be just fine."

"Perhaps," said Pooh, "we can tie a large piece of rope to the end of our string, and then pull it up to them once the string is there."

"I think we'd better go find a piece of rope," said Eeyore to Tigger, "before it starts to rain." And the two of them rushed off.

"Our Plan hasn't changed, has it, Pooh?" asked Piglet anxiously. He hoped it was still a Very Good Idea Piglet Plan.

"Not really," said Pooh. "We are just carrying out the refining and improving step."

"Is there anything we can do while we're waiting?" said Piglet.

"Owl? Can you fly the end of this string up to Rabbit and Roo and explain to them what our Plan is?"

"Certainly," said Owl, and he took the end of the string and began to fly up to the very top of the Ferris wheel.

He flew up and up, and as he got higher the string got longer and longer and heavier and heavier until, when he was very near the top, he had stopped flying up and was . . . stopped. Flying but stopped.

"What's happening?" squeaked Piglet.

"I think Owl is having trouble getting all the way to the top of the wheel," said Pooh.

"Well, he makes a very splendid kite," said Piglet, watching as Owl stopped flapping, and turned and glided down to land in front of them.

"I think . . . *puff* . . . *puff* . . . that the string . . . *puff* . . . *puff* . . . is too heavy . . . *puff* . . . *puff*. Necessary . . . *puff* . . . *puff* . . . Dorsal . . . *puff* . . . *puff* . . . Muscles . . . *puff* . . . *puff* . . . you know . . . *puff* . . . *puff*."

"Oh, Bother!" said Pooh. "Problems, problems, problems." And he sat down and tried to think. At that moment, Tigger bounced up, and Eeyore followed a moment later with a length of rope coiled on top of his back.

"We've found the rope!" bounced Tigger.

"And it's dry," said Eeyore, "though it won't be for long."

"We have another problem," said Piglet. "Owl cannot fly the string up to the top of the wheel because his Necessary Dorsal Muscles aren't enough so we can't get the string up to the top, so we can't tie the rope to it, so we can't pull the rope up, so we can't tie the rope to Rabbit and Roo and lower them down and rescue them!"

They all looked up again to the top of the wheel, where they saw the small figures again rocking and waving in the small seat. Several seagulls had perched on the top of the motionless wheel, and were sitting and staring at the curious pair.

"A kite!" shouted Pooh.

"Looks more like gulls to me," said Eeyore, squinting into the sun.

"No, no. I mean, perhaps we can use a kite to get the string up to them," said Pooh.

"That's a Very Good Idea, Pooh," said Piglet. "However did you think of it?"

"Well, I was thinking about changing plans on the fly, and that flies are much too small to be helpful with this, and then remembering when you said Owl looked like a kite up there, and then I thought about flying a kite, and how the string goes all the way up to the kite, much higher than the top of the wheel, and that's how I thought it . . . I think."

"Will it work?" asked Piglet. "Will it still be my 'Very Good Idea'?"

"Of course," said Pooh. "You had the original idea."

"Do we know where there's a kite?" asked Piglet.

"No."

"Oh."

I wish The Stranger would get back soon," said Pooh. "Perhaps he would know how to build a kite, or maybe where to find one."

"Maybe we can send up some balloons," said Piglet. "Like the time that you went after the honey in the honey tree. And then if Christopher Robin were here with his gun, he could shoot out the balloons and down they would drop."

"Too high," said Eeyore. "Much too high for Rabbit and Roo to drop, that is."

"But not if they were Jagulars," said Piglet, "who are Very Good Droppers."

"That's it!" said Pooh. "We shall do it!"

"Turn them into Jagulars?" said Tigger.

"No. Piglet has given me a Very Good Idea," said Pooh. "We shall make a kite out of balloons. We can tie one end of the string to the balloons and fly them up like a kite until they reach Rabbit and Roo. Then, they can grab the string and pull up the rope. And finally they can tie themselves to the rope and we'll all lower them down!"

It was very quiet as they all thought about Pooh's plan. It sounded like a Very Complex Plan when you heard it all at once, but each part of it had seemed so simple before. So surely it should work.

"Congratulations, Pooh!" said Piglet. "It is a Wonderful Plan."

So while Tigger went back to the balloon man to get some balloons for the kite, Owl flew up to Rabbit and Roo to explain the Plan, and Piglet and Pooh tied the string to the end of the rope. By now a small crowd of children had gathered around the base of the Ferris wheel and were watching them prepare their rescue. Tigger returned, bouncing even higher than usual due to the large bunch of balloons he was holding with one paw.

"Getting balloons is what Tiggers do best," he said.

"Now hold still, Tigger," said Piglet, "while I tie the balloons to the string."

Owl flew back down and landed lightly beside them.

"Are they ready?" asked Pooh. "And do they understand what they are to do?"

"They are currently resident in a state of high vigilance and anticipation," said Owl.

"Does that mean yes?" Pooh whispered to Piglet.

"It doesn't matter," said Eeyore, who had overheard. "We'd better try now anyway, before it starts to rain."

And their Plan worked just as they had thought.

Well, not quite. The balloons floated up in the breeze, just like a kite, but it was only after getting the knack of where the wind was coming from, that and unwrapping them from the odd tree or two, that they were able to get the string up to Rabbit and Roo. From then on the Plan worked just as they had thought.

Well, not quite. Rabbit forgot the part about untying the string from the balloons before they pulled the rope up, and Roo forgot the part about letting go of the string while they were pulling, so that they wound up with the rope halfway to the top of the wheel, and Roo halfway between Rabbit and the balloons, and the balloons halfway to the Forest before they noticed. Of course, after they got Roo down, and untied the balloons and pulled the rope up, from *then* on, the Plan worked just as they had thought.

Well, not quite. Eeyore wanted to be the anchor when they began to lower Rabbit and Roo, and so had asked Pooh to tie the rope to him so that he could walk slowly toward the wheel while the others held on and Rabbit and Roo were lowered to the ground. When Rabbit and Roo finally touched the ground, a cheer went up from the on-lookers who had gathered to watch the rescue.

Pooh and Piglet and Owl and Tigger let go of the rope and rushed over to meet them, and Eeyore, knowing the Rescue was over, wandered off toward the other tents. He had forgotten to undo the rope, and a moment later, Rabbit and Roo were lifted abruptly above their friends, and continued to rise, swinging back and forth until Piglet was able to convince Eeyore he should return. From *then* on, everything went just as they had thought.

Everyone praised Rabbit and Roo for their bravery, and Owl for his flying, Tigger for his finding and Eeyore for his pulling, and Piglet for his stopping Eeyore's pulling and his Very Good Idea. But most of all, they congratulated Pooh and one another for their Problem Solving by using SOLVE successfully.

The operator thanked them for getting Rabbit and Roo down from the top of the Ferris wheel and told them that when the repair crew had finished their work, they could come back and take all the free rides they wanted, although none of them except Roo really wanted to.

And when the onlookers began to drift away to ride the rides and see the sights, The Stranger returned.

"Is there a problem here?" asked The Stranger, carrying some popcorn and some other treats.

"No," said Pooh. "No problem at all."

X

In which the Problem-Solving Song Is Paraded and The Stranger Returns Home

Work on the Problem-Solving Book was finished, except for Writing It All Down, and The Stranger was leaving the Forest to begin that part of making a book.

Pooh felt that they should do the Customary and Proper thing.

"Piglet," Pooh said firmly, "we shall have a parade and music before The Stranger leaves."

So Pooh and Piglet got busy.

It was decided to have Rabbit organize the parade since he was used to coping with a large number of his smaller friends-and-relations and arranging them in a line so that they wouldn't get stepped on, which was pretty much the idea of a parade, according to Owl.

Rabbit agreed and after he got everyone's place properly set in his mind he gathered them all in a circle and told them exactly what each was to do.

Pooh, since he liked to make up songs, was in charge of the music part of the Celebration. He rehearsed everyone carefully until each knew his individual part and all could begin and end the music at the same time, or close enough so that it didn't matter. Even Eeyore, who was a Basso Profundo, thought the music was very good and appropriate for the beginning of an Important thing.

"Unless it rains," he said. "Then some lose their voices or get wheezles and sneezles in the middle of a note."

They had agreed to meet The Stranger at the edge of the Hundred Acre Wood before he left. Everyone from the Forest was there early: Pooh, Piglet, Rabbit, Tigger, Eeyore, Kanga, Roo, Small, and almost all of Rabbit's smaller friends-and-relations.

When The Stranger came along, the parade was all organized, and Rabbit gave the signal to start. It went very well with only a few minor problems like a collision in midair between Tigger and Kanga due to Tigger being carried away by the parade and being unable to restrain his bounciness.

Also Rabbit's smaller friends-and-relations tended to bunch up toward the end of the parade, and several times Eeyore had to warn Small about being stepped on, but afterward everyone agreed that it had undoubtedly been one of the finest parades ever held in the Hundred Acre Wood and certainly just as good as the one at the Fair.

At the end of the parade Pooh had instructed everyone to take their positions in the chorus for the music part of the Celebration. Piglet, Small, and most of Rabbit's smaller friends-and-relations were in the very front row, as they had the highest voices, and Eeyore was all alone in the back row, since he had the deepest voice.

Pooh stood out in front to lead because he knew the song best, having written it. He raised his arms and then brought them down, and almost everyone started to sing Pooh's Problem-Solving Song for The Stranger.

Select the problem of the day,
Finding one that's right to do,
You can choose it either way,
You pick it or it picks you.

Observe it very carefully,
"Where do I start? Where am I going?"
And don't forget about the bee,
"What's in the way of doing or knowing?"

Learn all you can by asking a lot,
But in the right order, as they are now,
Mostly Whys and then some Whats,
Then Where and When and Who and How.

(And after each, ask Why again.)

Vis-u-a-lize ideas, of course,
We think our thoughts and hope that they
Will put the cart behind the horse,
And not around the other way.

Employ the best idea found,
And watch what happens most precisely,
Making sure by looking 'round,
That things are working out quite nicely.

And for once, everybody, even Eeyore and Small, finished at the same time, and there was an echo which came back from the Hundred Acre Wood to add exactly the right touch.

There was silence for a moment and then The Stranger

was applauding and Pooh bowed and then applauded the chorus and soon everybody was applauding one another and then it was time to spread a blanket out and have lunch.

After lunch, the blanket that had been spread on the ground to eat lunch on was carefully cleaned of crumbs, inspected to make sure that none of Small's relatives were still clinging to it, and then folded away into The Stranger's basket.

First, of course, Pooh, being a Very Helpful Bear, had checked inside the basket to be certain that there was not the odd forgotten pot of honey or some of the little cake things with pink sugar icing there to make the basket heavier to carry than it had to be.

Finally, all the Good-byes had been said and then said again, just to make certain that everyone had his chance. The Thank-yous were very nicely offered and Good Lucks and Best Wishes were returned. Then it could not be put off any longer. They watched The Stranger walk away. He turned and waved one last time, disappearing into the trees.

They all waved back, except for Small and some of his relatives, who were so close to the ground that they had lost sight of The Stranger long ago. Besides, Small and some of his relatives were not properly shaped for waving, having six legs, and trying to decide which one to wave with caused them to become confused and fall about.

They all waited until the setting sun had almost sunk

behind the trees so that they were sure The Stranger was well on his way. Then the gathering slowly dispersed.

Pooh and Piglet walked home thoughtfully together in the golden evening, and for a long time they were silent.

"When you wake up in the morning, Pooh," said Piglet at last, "what's the first thing you say to yourself?"

"What's for breakfast?" said Pooh. "What do *you* say, Piglet?"

"I say I wonder what's going to happen exciting *to-day?*" said Piglet.

Pooh nodded thoughtfully.

"It's the same thing," he said.

Almost the first thing The Stranger did upon returning home was sit down and relax in the comfortable armchair that was just the right distance from the Very Nice Fire burning on the hearth. The first thing, of course, had been to light the fire, the wood having been properly arranged in the fireplace, ready for lighting.

Tomorrow, it would be necessary to begin the actual writing of *Winnie-the-Pooh on Problem Solving*, but now it was nice just to sit down without having to check whether one was sitting on a gorse bush or a thistle or Small or Alexander Beetle. That was a problem in the Forest, but not here.

However, there was one thing that was certain. There was no lack of problems outside the Forest that needed to be solved. One was constantly bombarded by them in the media.

There were the big problems affecting almost everyone in the world. For the most part they stemmed from wars, revolutions, disasters, disease, and social, cultural, and environmental change.

There were always many small Problems that were important primarily to the individuals trying to deal with their consequences. These were the stuff of talk shows, advice columns, and the thousands of how-to books.

Many problems were old ones that either had never been solved satisfactorily or had been solved in the past but had returned in a new form due to changing circumstances or conditions and needed to be solved again.

Some were brand-new problems, never before encountered by humanity.

Finding solutions to some of them was demonstrably a matter of Life or Death. In other cases the consequences were not as serious; failure to find a solution would only result in annoyance or inconvenience.

It is quite likely that most of these problems can be successfully solved using the methods presented in this book.

What is needed are more individuals who want to find solutions for problems, who can do it effectively, and who like the challenge. Those individuals could make things better, for themselves and for the world.

The Stranger thought about Winnie-the-Pooh, Piglet, Owl, Tigger, and the others in the Forest who had helped with the book and had grasped the idea of using the SOLVE Problem-Solving Method. They had demonstrated that at the Fair and had shown that they could apply it and use it on their own. The Stranger was pleased about that. If a bear and his friends could do that, almost anyone could.

All you need to do is learn the SOLVE Method and practice it on the problems that you select or that select you. Before long, you can say confidently as Pooh did:

"No. No problem at all."

POOH'S APPENDIX
Winnie-the-Pooh's
Problem-SOLVE-ing Checklist

Pooh is sometimes a Very Forgetful Bear, so he uses this. In case you are forgetful too (or you want to make certain you don't miss any steps using the SOLVE Method), he very nicely says you may use it also.

Select the Problem or Situation

- ❑ I selected It
- ❑ It selected me
- ❑ Chosen to Improve
  a process or situation
- ❑ Simple
- ❑ Complex
- ❑ Single
- ❑ Multiple

Emotional associations (if yes, characterize) Y or N
State the problem or situation as clearly and simply as you can

Observe, Organize, and Define the Problem or Situation

Starting place (any initial conditions, resources, current status)
Goal (desired end result upon successful completion)
Constraints (any limiting factors or obstacles)

Learn by Questioning All Parts of the Problem

Why solve it?	Why is it a problem?
What specifically is the problem?	
Where does the problem occur?	Why does it occur there?
When does the problem occur?	Why does it occur then?
Who is involved?	Why are they involved?
How does it happen?	Why does it happen that way?

Visualize Possible Solutions, Select One, and Refine It

Experience—Have you ever had a similar problem? How was that solved?

Approach:

❑ Numerical—numbers

❑ Analogy—similar item, process, idea

❑ Graphical—pics, graphs, diagrams

❑ Intuitive—gut feeling, hunch

❑ Logical—logic, deduction, inference

❑ Other

Idea Generators—Use to generate ideas *without* qualifying or judging them. Take the problem or a part of it and:

Make it bigger	Remove something
Make it smaller	Replace something with something else
Add something	Combine two elements
Take something away	Free association (say anything and see what comes to mind)
Exchange two parts	

Choose best solution—*Now*, be judgmental and review all ideas for the best one, list pluses and minuses for each, and feel free to combine, or modify.

Refine and improve—Review the selected idea carefully and improve or tweak.

Employ the Solution and Monitor Results

Action Plan—Create a path from here to there—list of all the things that need to be accomplished or gathered in sequence with timing and responsibilities noted.

Test on a small scale—If applicable, try out your solution a little at a time.

Employ and monitor—Put solution in place, and monitor criteria that will indicate success.

! If at last, the solution does not work, take heart—you may have received a very large and negative feedback, but you are still in the process of solving; just repeat all the above steps using what you now know as additional input.

· A NOTE ON THE TYPE ·

The typeface used in this book is a version of Goudy (Old Style), originally designed by Frederick W. Goudy (1865–1947), perhaps the best known and certainly one of the most prolific of American type designers, who created over a hundred typefaces—the actual number is unknown because a 1939 fire destroyed many of his drawings and "matrices" (molds from which type is cast). Initially a calligrapher, rather than a type cutter or printer, he represented a new breed of designer made possible by late-nineteenth-century technological advance; later on, in order to maintain artistic control, he supervised the production of matrices himself. He was also a tireless promoter of wider awareness of type, with the paradoxical result that the distinctive style of his influential output tends to be associated with his period and, though still a model of taste, can now seem somewhat dated.

· A NOTE ON THE TYPE ·

The typeface used in this book is a version of Goudy (Old Style), originally designed by Frederick W. Goudy (1865–1947), perhaps the best known and certainly one of the most prolific of American type designers, who created over a hundred typefaces—the actual number is unknown because a 1939 fire destroyed many of his drawings and "matrices" (molds from which type is cast). Initially a calligrapher, rather than a type cutter or printer, he represented a new breed of designer made possible by late-nineteenth-century technological advance; later on, in order to maintain artistic control, he supervised the production of matrices himself. He was also a tireless promoter of wider awareness of type, with the paradoxical result that the distinctive style of his influential output tends to be associated with his period and, though still a model of taste, can now seem somewhat dated.